Greek Culture and the Greek Testament

BY THE SAME AUTHOR

PAUL AND HIS EPISTLES
JOHN AND HIS WRITINGS
THE SYNOPTIC GOSPELS AND THE BOOK OF ACTS
NEW TESTAMENT EPISTLES
THE GIFT OF TONGUES
GREAT CHARACTERS OF THE NEW TESTAMENT
THE MOST BEAUTIFUL BOOK EVER WRITTEN

Greek Culture and the Greek Testament

A Plea for the Study of the Greek Classics
and the Greek New Testament

By
DOREMUS A. HAYES
Chair of New Testament Interpretation,
Graduate School of Theology,
Evanston, Illinois

WIPF & STOCK · Eugene, Oregon

Wipf and Stock Publishers
199 W 8th Ave, Suite 3
Eugene, OR 97401

Greek Culture and the Greek Testament
A Plea for the Study of the Greek Classics
and the Greek New Testament
By Hayes, Doremus A.
Softcover ISBN-13: 978-1-6667-3353-2
Hardcover ISBN-13: 978-1-6667-2824-8
Publication date 8/5/2021
Previously published by The Abingdon Press, 1925

This edition is a scanned facsimile of
the original edition published in 1925.

To
ERNEST WARD BURCH
ABLE SCHOLAR, DEVOTED TEACHER, LOYAL
ASSOCIATE IN THE NEW TESTAMENT FIELD

CONTENTS

	PAGE
A PERSONAL FOREWORD	9

PART
I. A WONDERFUL LAND.................. 11
II. A WONDERFUL PEOPLE................ 19
III. A WONDERFUL LANGUAGE............. 66
IV. A WONDERFUL LITERATURE..... 110
V. A WONDERFUL BOOK. THE GREATEST GREEK BOOK: THE NEW TESTAMENT 152

A PERSONAL FOREWORD

FOR some years early in life I held the chair of Greek Language and Literature in a college faculty. For many years now I have worked in the department of New Testament Interpretation in a theological school. All of my teaching career has been devoted to a study of the Greek, and my life has been indefinitely enriched thereby. This little book is written in the hope that others may be induced to share in the privileges I have enjoyed.

I hear to-day that one of my neighbors has begun the study of Greek in a correspondence course. Years ago she heard Professor Gildersleeve lecture on the advantages of Greek culture and ever since she has longed to study Greek for herself. She had no opportunity in middle life; but now in her widowhood and the comparative leisure of advancing years she is realizing her cherished ambition at last. She is at present reading the Anabasis with great delight and we can imagine what her joy will be when she comes to the reading of her Greek New Testament.

Within the week I have heard of another of

my neighbors who when sent to Arizona in ill health was warned by his physicians not to take many books with him; and so he took only one book, his Greek Testament. Will anyone who reads this volume be disposed to question the wisdom of his choice?

I desired to call this book *Gold and White Ivory,* taking the words from one of Pindar's Odes to represent what was valuable and to be had only for effort and cost; but the publishers thought that the title was too blind, and they preferred the prosier and plainer one now given. One must dig for gold. One must travel far to find original ivory. Yet there are those who think it worth while and who come home laden with rich treasure. Are there not many, both among the laity and the clergy, who will be willing to toil as much as may be necessary in order to enjoy the reward of personal and first-hand acquaintance with Greek Culture and the Greek Testament? When they once realize its value and its necessity, I am assured that they will. I have written in that faith and to that end.

Evanston, June 1, 1925.

PART I

A WONDERFUL LAND

1. THE land of the Greeks was and is a most remarkable land. Its most noteworthy feature is its remarkable coast line. No other land has anything like it. The continent of Africa is an almost solid mass, presenting an unbroken front to the sea. Africa prefers to sit out on desert sands and sun herself. She is the Dark Continent; and her people are black. It is small wonder; she hates the water so. Africa has but one mile of coast line for every six hundred and twenty-three square miles of surface. On the other hand the continent of Europe loves the sea. She runs out in great peninsulas to meet it, and hugs it to her in great gulfs. She has one mile of coast line for every one hundred and fifty-six square miles of surface.

"As the configuration of Europe contrasts with that of Africa, the configuration of Greece contrasts with and surpasses in its complexity even that of Europe. The coast of Greece is a continuous succession of bays, pressing in upon the land at every possible point from the east and the west and the south. Everywhere peninsulas run out into the sea; everywhere the sea thrusts itself in between these projecting points of land. Half the size of Portugal, Greece has a coast line greater than Spain and Portugal together."[1] Greece proper is smaller than the State of Pennsylvania, but "its coast line is almost as long as the whole Atlantic seaboard of the United States from Maine to Florida."[2] The sea is on every side of the land and in every part of the land. There is not a foot of land in Greece which is more than forty miles from the sea.

2. Another noteworthy feature of the land is to be found in the multitude of its mountains. No land is richer in mountain peaks. Nearly nine tenths of its surface is covered with mountain ranges. There is no spot in the land which is more than ten miles away from the hills. Along the major part of our Atlantic coast, while we have the ocean, the mountains are a long way off. In Colorado and Wyoming we have the Rocky Mountains, but the sea is far, far away. In the great flat country of the central valley and the desert

---

[1] Hayes, *Paul and His Epistles*, p. 189.
[2] Greene, *The Achievement of Greece*, p. 15. Harvard University Press. Used by permission.

and the prairies life may become flat and monotonous too. California is the one great State of our Union which has both the mountains and the sea. It does not compare with Greece in this respect, but in many places you can be within sight of salt water and at the same time within sight of lofty mountain peaks. The white-capped breakers and the snow-capped summits keep the air vital all the time. Greece is the ideal land in this respect. It has more mountains and more sea to the square mile than any other land on the globe. Not even Japan can compare with it.

3. A third noteworthy and peculiar feature of the land is to be found in its climate. Mountains and sea are in close proximity in the fiords of Norway and in the volcanic regions of the South Seas; but no one would think of these as ideal homes for the human race. Greece, like every mountainous country in the south, has every variety of climate represented in the various zones of mountain height; but more than most other countries it has a remarkable variety of climate in its valleys and on its level plains. Gell says that in traveling through the Morea in March he found summer in Messenia, spring in Laconia, and winter in Arcadia, inside a radius of fifty miles; and Curtius tells us that within a boundary of not

more than two degrees of latitude, the land of Greece reaches from the beeches of Pindus into the climate of the palm; and on the entire known surface of the globe there is no other region in which the different zones of climate and flora meet one another in so rapid a succession.[3]

The land of the Greeks was a land of sunshine, full of sweetness and light. On the whole the climate tended to cheerfulness and was a constant stimulus to the cultivation of all the civilized arts. At Athens, after observations extending over twenty-four years, the director of the Observatory there reports that there are on the average in the year one hundred and seventy-nine clear days, on which the sun is not hid for a moment, one hundred and fifty-seven days which are bright days, on which the sun is hid perhaps for half an hour, twenty-six cloudy days, and only three days in which the sun is not seen at all.

Neumann and Partsch[4] tell us that the average number of sunny days in Germany is seventy-nine in the year; seventy-nine days of sunshine as against three hundred and thirty-six in Athens! With the fogs of England and the mists of Scotland it is not likely that they

---
[3] Curtius, *History of Greece*, vol. i, p. 11.
[4] *Physikalisch Geographie von Griechenland*, p. 24.

THE GREEK TESTAMENT 15

would make a better showing than Germany in this regard, and other European countries would be more or less like them; and we are not surprised that Herodotus, who was a great traveler in Asia and Africa, came to the conclusion that beyond all other countries in the world Greece had the most happily tempered seasons, and that other good authorities like Aristotle and Hippocrates agreed with him. One needs only to visit Greece, and then go on to Palestine and Egypt to-day, to sympathize fully with their verdict in that matter.

Aristotle was the closest observer of his age and a man of encyclopedic information, and he averred that the peoples in the colder regions of Europe in his day were energetic but lacking in intelligence and artistic skill, while the Asiatics were intelligent and artistic enough but they were wanting in the energy that characterized the inhabitants of a colder clime; but the Greeks, living geographically between the two, had the energy of the one and the intelligence and artistry of the other. It is true that their land had the ideal climate for study and work. The energies of its people "were neither lethargized by excessive heat nor paralyzed by excessive cold."[5] Their

---

[5]*Makers of Hellas*, p. 24. Charles Scribner's Sons. Used by permission.

heads could be as clear as their skies all the year round. Their mental powers were neither melted in summer nor frozen in winter. Their climate did all it could for them in keeping them in good working condition week after week, month after month, year after year.

4. A fourth feature in the situation of this remarkable land ought to be mentioned. It was the natural center of the ancient world. Reclus, the geographer, has said: "The axes of civilization in the western extremity of Asia converge upon the basin of the Hellenic Mediterranean. The long fissure of the Red Sea points directly toward the Eastern Mediterranean. The winding valley of the Nile opens in the same direction. The Persian Gulf, continued to the northwest by the Euphrates, runs toward that angle of the Mediterranean where is Cyprus. Farther north all the rivers, all the highways of commerce which descend from Asia Minor, from the continent of Asia, from the Sarmatian plains to the Black Sea, become tributaries to the Greek waters through the Bosphorus and Hellespont."[6]

Such was this land; surrounded by sunny waters, filled with mountain fastnesses, with the ideal climate for either pleasure or exertion, and in the focal center of the civiliza-

[6]Contemporary Review, October, 1894.

tions of the three great continents of the ancient world. "The southeastern extremity of Europe, Hellas lies, as it were, between three worlds. Opposite stretch the most fertile parts of Africa—the Egypt of ancient days, with its mysterious religion, its curious art and learning. Nearer, across a sea studded with chains of islands, each of which, in the infancy of navigation, served as a stepping-stone to the mariner, lie the shores of Asia, the home of the earliest civilization. To the west, separated only by waters whose breadth in some places does not exceed forty miles, is Italy, in these old times the representative of unexplored regions beyond. Thus stood Hellas, between the Old World and the New—the gateway, as it were, through which the primitive knowledge of the East was to enter upon a fresh and more vigorous life of progress in the West."[7]

Greece is one of the three peninsulas of Southern Europe. On the map the westernmost, Spain, looks like a clenched fist, ready to crush or maul its subject peoples in the Netherlands, in Mexico, in the Philippines, in Cuba, in Peru. The middle peninsula, Italy, looks on the map like a giant foot or boot, kicking at Sicily first of all, but ready to set itself upon the neck of a conquered world.

[7] *Makers of Hellas*, p. 13.

The peninsula of Greece on the map has been likened to a mulberry leaf or the webbed foot of a duck, but these comparisons are so inadequate that we are tempted to suggest that it is more like an open palm with the fingers extending everywhither or possibly still more like the corrugated surface of a human brain.

In physical conformation it might stand on the map for a symbol of acquisitiveness and intellectuality, of open-handedness and open-mindedness, of a desire for personal possession only that it may impart its riches to all the world. Spain was selfish, and died as a world power long ago. Rome was selfish, and its world empire passed into other hands. Greece controls the life and dominates the thought of the world to-day.

Environment has something to do with the development of any people. Geographical situation may not account wholly for national characteristics; but under such unprecedentedly favorable conditions for the development of a race as were furnished by the commanding position, the air, the soil, and the safe harbors on the many seas of Greece, we naturally would expect the development of a unique and wonderful people.

PART II

A WONDERFUL PEOPLE

1. *Pioneers and Discoverers.* We are considering the ancient Greeks in this discussion, the Greeks of the primitive and then of the classical periods, the Greeks of the early and then of the Great Age. The early Greeks lived upon the sea as much as upon the land. The quiet waters of the bays tempted them from the shore; the outlying islands were so near at hand that the most inexperienced mariners might venture there; and as island upon island rose upon the horizon they found themselves led by easy stages to the three continents from whose varied products they might enrich themselves.

As Curtius says, "Scarcely a single point is to be found between Asia and Europe where, in clear weather, a mariner would feel himself left in a solitude between sky and water; the eye reaches from island to island, and easy voyages of a day lead from bay to bay."[1] While the other Aryan peoples of Europe had

[1] Curtius, *op. cit.*, vol. 1, p. 10.

no other name for the sea than "the barren," "the waste," "the dead water," the Greeks called it "the bridge" or "the pathway." To them the sea was no barrier between them and other peoples. It was the highroad uniting them to all.

Almost perforce, therefore, the Greeks became mariners, world-wanderers, discoverers. Their horizon was broadened and they came to have wider interests and a wider knowledge than the stay-at-home peoples had. The sea did that for them. They came to be a people of cosmopolitan outlook and of encyclopedic information. They were "the world's greatest pioneers and experimenters," and we are assured that on the basis of their experiments more than half the culture of the modern world rests. The Greeks were both mountaineers and mariners; and it has been suggested that their mountains helped them to be maintainers of the old and the sea made them seekers after the new. They were conservative of the substantial and the good, and consumedly eager for new and better things.

2. *Lovers of liberty.* Mountaineers always are lovers of liberty. The Greeks were no exception to the rule. They always were ready to fight, bleed, and die for freedom. Patriotism and independence always were character-

istic of the race. In our histories Salamis, Marathon, and Thermopylæ almost have become synonyms for these terms. The people on the plains are open to every assault, and if overrun by superior numbers they easily are swept into great empires; but the people in the mountain passes are not overcome so readily. Sometimes a handful of men there can hold a whole army at bay.

The mountains made of Greece a natural fortress, shielded on the west and on the north. Shut in on every side the population of each mountain valley had to be independent. It was a difficult journey to the next neighbors across the peaks. Isolation and liberty went together; and together they were cherished and loved. To conquer such a land every mountain valley had to be mastered in succession. If one of them was left unvisited, it became the refuge and the rallying-place of the surviving friends of liberty.

Patriotism is fostered most easily among mountain peaks. What would the Swiss care for Switzerland minus the Alps? The spirits of the mountaineer flag upon the prairies or the plains. He feels smothered there. He pines for the ozone of the heights. He loves to dwell in memory upon the rocks and "templed hills." He sings,

"My country! 'tis of thee,
Sweet land of liberty,
  Of thee I sing:
Land where my fathers died!
. . . .
From every *mountain* side
Let *freedom* ring!"

The Greeks were characterized equally by love of their native land and love of liberty. They were independent in their thought and speech and life, original in their literature, vital and varied and unrestrained in everything. They invented politics, and they perfected the conceptions of law and liberty, justice and democracy, parliament and public opinion. They felt the need of these things and went to work upon their development with the same thoroughness and genius they gave to their literature and their art.

3. *Moral and Religious.* Mountaineers are rigidly and ruggedly religious. To the Greeks the gods dwelt everywhere; but the home of Zeus and the chief court of all divinities was on Mount Olympus. Greece reached outward in all directions toward the continents and into the sea; and Greece reached upward in her innumerable mountain peaks toward the purer atmosphere and into the clear sky. So the Greeks ever were reaching outward to the

THE GREEK TESTAMENT 23

uttermost parts of the earth in the acquisition of spiritual knowledge and material wealth; and they ever were reaching upward to the uttermost possibilities of human achievement and aspiration. It was a question to which they owed the more, the inspirations of the mountains or the invitations of the sea.

Their religion had in it the freedom of the open air. There was nothing depressing about it. They had no religious austerities or monasteries. They never indulged in fastings or flagellations. Their religion was a natural and a joyous one. Their faith was cheerful, facing either life or death. The Ceramicus, their cemetery, was filled with artistic monuments without a word of terror or despair inscribed upon them. Their sorrow was sincere but serene. Excessive mourning was forbidden by law. Their faith did not fail them in the last hour. They were not afraid of death, because their consciences were clear in life.

They were a highly moral people when their race was at its prime. As John Fiske says, "They had an open, childlike, sunny conception of religion"; and "their moral and religious life sat easily upon them like their own graceful garments."[2] In an article on "The

---
[2]Martin, *Is Mankind Advancing?* p. 172. Used by permission of the author.

Ethical Value of Hellenism" Mr. Alfred W. Benn has said, "I am prepared to support the thesis that the Greeks were as great in what belongs to the conduct of life as they confessedly were in the creation of beauty or in the search for truth. . . . The moral life of no other people was so rich, so well-balanced."[3] They excelled morally and artistically.

The Greeks practiced monogamy and abhorred polygamy at the time when the Hebrews still were a polygamous people. Long before Jesus had given the Golden Rule to his disciples, "All things therefore whatsoever ye would that men should do unto you, even so do ye also unto them,"[4] Isocrates in his Nicocles had taught the Greeks not to do to others that which would make them angry if others should do it to them. In the Crito Socrates concludes, "We ought not to retaliate or render evil for evil to anyone, whatever evil we may have suffered from him,"[5] and he manifested the same spirit and meant the same thing with the Master on the Mount. Long before the days of Socrates, Pittacus of Mitylene had said, "Forgiveness is better than revenge," and "Speak no evil of a friend, or

---

[3] International Journal of Ethics, April, 1902.
[4] Matt. 7. 12.
[5] *Crito*, 49C.

THE GREEK TESTAMENT 25

even of an enemy."[6] No higher standards of speech and conduct are enunciated in our Gospels.

Long before that young prophet of Nazareth said to his disciples, "Ye have heard that it was said, An eye for an eye, and a tooth for a tooth; but I say unto you, Resist not him that is evil,"[7] Lycurgus the lawgiver had illustrated the spirit of that command by his personal example. His eye was put out by an angry young man and instead of taking vengeance upon the ruffian Lycurgus took him to his own home and there reasoned with him with such cogency of argument and such courtesy of conduct that the young man was converted from an enemy into a friend, and we read that he became "a most decorous and discreet man."[8]

Modern theology has not transcended the moral notions of Æschylus and his school. He censured high-handedness even in the gods. He taught the indelible nature of sin. The Greek drama in the hands of Æschylus and Sophocles and Euripides served the purposes of the modern pulpit in being the greatest elevating and moralizing influence in the land.

[6]Diogenes Laertius, i, 76, 78.
[7]Matt. 5. 38, 39.
[8]Plutarch, *Lycurgus*, xi.

The immorality characteristic of many performances on the modern stage never was tolerated among the Greeks.

Euripides describes the conditions in Athens in the following words:

"The weak, the rich, have here one equal right,
And penury, with justice on its side,
Triumphs o'er riches; this is to be free.
Is there a mind that teems with noble thought
And useful to the state? He speaks his thought
And is illustrious. When a people free
Are sovereigns of their land, the state stands firm."[9]

We give much praise to the Hebrew prophets for their passionate preaching of civic righteousness and social justice; but it is well for us to remember that at the very time they were saying these things, "there were established righteous governments in Greece under which the poor working man could not be plundered with impunity as he was in the Holy Land. Unaided by supernatural promises or terrors, the Greek legislators, magistrates, and orators actually accomplished that for which the Hebrew prophets vainly strove."

To the Greek sin was ugly, but there was something fine in high behavior. The beautiful always appealed to him and noble conduct

---

[9] Euripides, *Suppliants*, 399f.

THE GREEK TESTAMENT

was a thing of beauty in which he rejoiced. He was moral and religious not because he was afraid of the law of the state or the wrath of the gods but because he loved the true, the beautiful, and the good. It was the Greek ideal which Paul put before the Philippians when he wrote to them, "Finally, brethren, whatsoever things are true, whatsoever things are honorable, whatsoever things are just, whatsoever things are pure, whatsoever things are lovely, whatsoever things are gracious; if there be any virtue, and if there be any praise, think on these things."[10] The whole Epistle to the Philippians is characterized by a graciousness of manner and a cheerfulness of spirit and a joyousness of religious faith which would be attractive to any Greek community, and this exhortation to think upon things gracious, lovely, pure, just, honorable, and true simply emphasized the ideals of their own philosophers and their own national life.

The religious spirit of the Greek finds its classical expression in the prayer with which Plato closes the Phædrus: "O beloved Pan and other gods here present, grant to me to become fair within. Let my outward possessions be such as are favorable to my inward life. May I think the wise man rich. Give me

[10]Phil. 4. 8.

so much gold as only the temperate man can bear or carry. . . . O beloved Pan, grant me to become fair within."[11] That sums it up; plain living, high thinking, and the beauty of holiness within.

Hippocrates, about 400 B. C., was the founder of medical science among the Greeks, and he illustrates well the spirit of religion which the Greek carried into all of his work. The Hippocratic oath, taken by all the practitioners of his school, contained the following pledges: "I will give no deadly medicine to anyone if asked, nor suggest any such counsel; nor will I aid a woman to produce abortion. With purity and holiness I will pass my life and practice my art." This high ideal helped to maintain the dignity of the medical profession among the Arabs, Jews, and Christians through all the succeeding centuries. It illustrates the religious spirit maintained by the Greeks in all their professions and arts.

4. *Devoted to the Ideal.* Highly favored by climatic and geographical conditions the Greeks made the most of their opportunities and realized their possibilities in fuller measure than any other nation did. Professor Butcher, in his volume, *Some Aspects of the Greek Genius,* has summarized the character-

---
[11]Plato, *Phædrus*, 279B.

istics of the Greek people under the four heads: (1) A love of knowledge for its own sake, a passion for truth, and for seeing things as they really are, with no care for consequences. (2) A strong belief in conduct—such "noble action" as might be becoming to "clear thought." (3) A mastery of art, such as still sets its models for the world—art also being loved for its own sake, and its chief excellences being the absence of exaggeration, the delicate spirit of choice, the unobtrusive propriety of diction. (4) A passionate demand and assertion of political freedom. These were the "Gifts of Greece," which gave her the right to the name of "The Holy Land of the Ideal."

It is a lofty title. To try to reach the ideal has seemed to the most of us to be an attempt at the impossible; and we moderns are for the most part tamely content with second-best things. It was not so with the Greeks. They constantly were striving for the realization of the ideal; and it may be well for us moderns, with our growing contempt for the ancients and our increasing neglect of the classic models and the classic times, to remember that in Greece, in science and philosophy, in literature and art, there has been the most complete realization of the ideal all-around human life of a nation which the world as yet has seen.

Our Christian religion comes to us directly from Judaism but it has been greatly modified for the better by its contact with Greek influences. The humanistic elements of Hellenism were in fullest accord with the spirit of Jesus. It believed with him that God and man were much alike in their nature. It rejoiced in the beauty of the universe and the comeliness and charm of all created things. It was broader-minded than Judaism and more appreciative of the immanence of God and the unlimited possibilities of man. This faith in the continual presence of God and the undefined and undefinable powers of man led the Greeks to strive for better things and to be content with nothing but the ultimate best. Their ideal was perfection and their constant endeavor toward it made Greece at last The Holy Land of the Ideal.

This is so patently true that among the students of Greek antiquity, the archæologists and philologists, the historians of their art, their literature, and their nation, the tendency seems to be toward an enthusiastic and almost unlimited idealism. We turn from the reading of their volumes with the more or less positive impression that classic Greece must

THE GREEK TESTAMENT

have been blessed with an Edenic loveliness of landscape and life. They must have had storms sometimes, there must have been dark days; but for the most part we have the vision of a cloudless heaven, of a fathomless blue sky overarching the fathomless blue of the summer sea, of Olympian heights where gods might dwell in boundless light and in perfect peace, of Arcadian vales where nymphs and fauns and dryads might find fit frolicking place.

5. *Beautiful in Form.* This perfect beauty of sky and shore and sea was reflected in the forms of the Greek women and men; in the Apollo Belvederian symmetry and strength of the naked youths of the gymnasium, in the Venus-de-Milo grace and loveliness of the Penelopes and Aspasias and Helens, the maids and mothers of this favored race; in the serene stateliness of the Greek warriors and artists and lawgivers and philosophers; in the beauty of an Alcibiades, the dignity of a Pericles, the surpassing symmetry in feature and form in a favorite poet like Sophocles; in the only less ideal figures and carriage of the great populace which formed in religious processions like that displayed upon the matchless frieze of the Parthenon.

We shall not soon forget the certainty of enthusiastic conviction with which Ernst

Curtius, the poet-archæologist and the great historian of Greece, told us in his classroom in Berlin that "ugliness was the rare exception among the Greeks; they were the people of perfect form. . . . They were freer than other mortal races from all that hinders and oppresses the motions of the mind. . . . With other nations beauty, with the Greeks want of beauty, was the startling exception to the rule." Professor Gulick, in his *Life of the Ancient Greeks,* agrees with Professor Curtius at this point. He says, "The Greeks produced a larger proportion of handsome men and women than any people who have ever lived. They were tall and well proportioned, having firm skin and supple muscles, well-formed heads, straight noses, and brown hair. Above all, they were noted for their extraordinarily beautiful eyes, possessing a keen and steady gaze."[12]

Ridpath is as enthusiastic as either of these authorities we have quoted, and, if possible, he is even more so. He declares, "In beauty of body the Greeks were peerless; in agility and nervous vigor they were the finest whom the world has produced. The Greek was more alive than any man of antiquity. This highly

---
[12]Gulick, *Life of the Ancient Greeks,* p. 171. D. Appleton & Co. Used by permission.

THE GREEK TESTAMENT 33

wrought physical manhood was the foundation of his wonderful mind, of his energy, his reason, his imagination, his courage. In Greece nature accomplished the finest motherhood of man. In the fair skin, blue eyes, beautiful body, and radiant face of the Greek youth she held aloft the best gift of her abundant love. No other people were so greatly gifted with personal beauty and none other ever so adored the gift."[13] We might change the last clause in one word and say that no other people so adorned the gift. Beauty and brains do not always go together; but they did with the Greeks.

Ugly people are common enough among us. Beautiful people rarely are seen. It was just the other way among the Greeks. As a nation they preserved the golden mean in their physique. Generally speaking, there were no giants among them, and no dwarfs; no excessively corpulent people and no people excessively thin. As a rule, they enjoyed health of body and beauty of form and vigor of physique. Socrates in his ugliness of features was the outstanding exception among the great men of Greek history. It always was a puzzle to the Greeks how so noble a spirit could inhabit so ignoble a form. Socrates him-

---
[13]Martin, *op. cit.*, p. 103.

self used to advise young men to look at themselves often in the mirror. "If you are handsome," he said, "make yourselves worthy of your looks; if you have the misfortune to be ugly, use high accomplishments for a veil."[14] Surely, no man ever practiced more faithfully than Socrates what he preached.

Herophilos, physician and philosopher, voiced the faith of his people when he declared that "Science and Art have equally nothing to show, Strength is incapable of effort, Wealth useless, and Eloquence powerless if Health be wanting." The Greeks were devoted to gymnastics and "setting-up" exercises. Their physical health and their mental strength and their bodily beauty largely were due to their simple diet and their simple habits of life. They did not merely talk about the simple life; they lived it. They spent most of their time in the open air. They had no steam-heated houses. They had one simple garment, or in cold weather two. They had no store clothes and no fashionable tailors. They wore sandals or shoes of soft leather, or they went barefooted and unashamed.

Boeckh, in his *Public Economy of Athens,* says that Socrates seems to have had one pair of dress shoes which lasted him for a lifetime.

---

[14] Diogenes Laertius, II, 16 33.

He regarded shoes as an effeminacy, and in the Thracian campaign he trudged barefoot over the icy battlefields. One only can imagine what he would have thought and have said if he could have seen the high-heeled French shoes and the tight-laced French corsets some modern women wear. Socrates used to say that, as it is the attribute of God to want nothing, so to want as little as possible comes the nearest to God.[15] It is told of him that he walked down the street of Athens and saw the many articles of food and merchandise, and thanked God with all sincerity that there were so many things which he could get along without. Yet even he was taunted by Diogenes as a luxurious man. Diogenes said, "You have a cottage and a truck-bed and sometimes, when you dine out, you put on a pair of shoes!"[16] Polycrates gave Anacreon a large sum of money and Anacreon lay awake two nights thinking about his wealth. Then he returned it to Polycrates, saying that it was not worth the anxiety it occasioned.[17]

There were no slums in Athens, no apartment houses, and no tenements. They had no whisky there and no rum or gin or beer. They

---

[15] Stobæus, *Flor.*, V, 35.
[16] Ælian, *Var. Hist.*, IV, 11.
[17] Stobæus, *Flor.*, XC, 25.

had no confectioners' shops, and the only sweetmeats they had were cakes baked with honey. They had no coffee and no tea and no cocoa and no spices and no lard. They lived without hot biscuits and fried grease and the deadly pie. They had none of these things, but they did have fine complexions and clear heads and bright eyes. The best Greeks would have considered us too self-indulgent in our eating and in our living. They were more frugal and hardy in their habits than we. They lived as simply as those first disciples of Jesus.

They had no love either for riches or for luxury. A meal without sugar and without pepper and without coffee and without cordials of any kind was sufficient both for their appetites and their tastes. They drank goats' milk and sheep's milk and with their meals they had wine diluted with two or three parts water. A little milk and a few dates were sufficient to stay their hunger, and they considered it a feast if they had a loaf of bread and a jug of wine with a head of lettuce and some nuts. They ate both leavened and unleavened bread, fruits, olives, nuts, salads, vegetables, raisins, figs, fish, and flesh. They had no cigars or tobacco. Epicurus said that barley cakes and water were sufficient for his needs and that he could live on one obulus a day.

THE GREEK TESTAMENT 37

An obulus would represent about twelve or fifteen cents in our money.

Herodotus tells us that when Xerxes fled from Greece he left all his costly dinner service of plate to Mardonius, and, after the death of Mardonius at Platæa, Pausanius ordered the cooks to prepare a dinner precisely as they would have done it for Mardonius. Then he had his own servants prepare a Spartan dinner and spread it by the side of the other. Calling in his own generals, he laughed heartily at the contrast between the two, and he said, "Gentlemen, I wished to point out to you the folly of the Persian general, who with all this grandeur came to rob you of your miserable meal."[18] Gold and silver and luxury on the one side and nothing but the plainest of food and the simplest of service on the other; and it was to the plain living that the victory had been given.

It was a common saying in Athens that those who dined with Plato never had a headache the following morning. His fare was so frugal that it rendered repentance for overindulgence an impossibility. Timotheus, the son of Conon, had dinner with Plato in the Academy. He had been used to costly banquets and he felt so much better the following

[18]Herodotus, ix, 82.

day that he said to Plato when he next met him, "You philosophers dine better for tomorrow than for to-day."[19] Plato must have appreciated that remark. When he himself saw that there were people in Agrigentum who had costly houses and gave costly banquets he remarked that they built as if they were to live forever, and dined as if they would be dead forever.[20] "The poor Athenian with his barley loaf and a handful of olives and a draught of plentifully-diluted wine was as happy as any king."[21]

In the Republic of Plato Socrates describes the manner of life of its citizens and he says: "They will feed on barley and wheat, baking the wheat and kneading the flour, making noble puddings and loaves. . . . But, said Glaucon, interposing, you have not given them a relish to their meal. True, I replied, I had forgotten that; of course they will have a relish—salt, and olives, and cheese, and onions, and cabbages and other country herbs which are fit for boiling; and we shall give them a dessert of figs, and pulse, and beans, and myrtle-berries, and beech-nuts, which they will roast at the fire, drinking in moderation.

---
[19] Athen., x, p. 419.
[20] Ælian, *Var. Hist.*, xii, 29.
[21] *Makers of Hellas*, p. 34.

And with such a diet they may be expected to live in peace to a good old age, and bequeath a similar life to their children after them."[22] This was the Socratic idea of plain and sufficient living.

It is not to be supposed that all the Greeks kept closely to such a regimen in their diet, but it is a fact that they seldom or never broke down nervously, and many of them lived so healthfully that they attained to a remarkable old age, even as Socrates had suggested. "Plato died at eighty-two and was occupied intellectually to his last hour. Isocrates wrote his *Panathenæsus* at ninety-four. His teacher, Gorgias, lived to be one hundred. When someone asked him how he managed to live so long, he said, 'By never eating or doing anything merely for pleasure.'[23] Chrysippus wrote on logic at seventy-two. Cleanthes taught up to his ninety-ninth year. Sophocles wrote his *Œdipus at Colonus,* one of the greatest tragedies ever composed, when he was ninety years old.

"Diogenes lived to be ninety, and he worked away in his latter years as diligently as when he was younger, and when his friends begged

---

[22]Jowett, *The Dialogues of Plato*, vol. ii, p. 194. Charles Scribner's Sons. Used by permission.

[23]Stobæus, *Flor.* c, 21.

him to relax a little he said, 'If I had run the long course in a race, would you have said, Do slack your pace a little at the end?'[24] Hippocrates seems to have been able to obey the mandate to physicians, 'Heal thyself,' for he lived to be one hundred and four. Cratinus, the comic poet, died at ninety-seven. Pindar, the poet, lived to be eighty; Simonides, eighty-nine; Pyrrho, ninety; Timon, ninety; Xenocrates, eighty-two. Xenophon lived to be over ninety; Zeno, the Stoic philosopher, died at ninety-eight, while Anacreon, the poet of beauty, love, and wine, lived to the age of eighty-five and then described himself as a cheerful, joyous old man."[25]

Matthew Arnold has contrasted the Hebraic and the Hellenic ideals of life in the following words: "The difference is indeed striking between the narrow and the fierce absorption of the Jew in the fortunes of his nation, his indifference to all but concrete tangible marks of Divine favor, his intense will-power and defective æsthetic sensibility, and (on the other side) the genial, open-minded mentality of the Greek, full of curiosity and the enjoyment of nature, an artist to his finger-tips, as the Japanese, and no other nation, are to-day;

---

[24] Diog Laert, vi, 2 34
[25] Martin, *op. cit.*, pp. 104-105.

whose religion was a poetical and symbolical mythology; who lived in a present which he loved to enjoy and ardently desired to understand; who, like a child, craved only to see all that is to be seen of this wonderful world and the spiritual mysteries which may lie behind it; whose intellect was so much more developed than his will that he sincerely believed that to see the truth was to possess it, vice being only ignorance and virtue knowledge; and whose sense of the finer values of life was so keen that he frankly despised unnecessary apparatus, and lived a hardier and a healthier life than any civilized race has lived before or since."

That closing statement summarizes all we have said on this portion of our subject. The Greek minds and muscles were developed equally and perfectly, and that made them preeminent among the races of men.

6. *Artistic in Everything.* The savants have given us to understand that the beauty of nature in Greece and the beauty of physique among the Greeks were transcended by the perfect beauty of their language and their literature, their poetry and their philosophy, their architecture, their sculpture, and their art. One of them has suggested that while the subjective arts of poetry and music were pro-

vided with a perfect organ in the Greek tongue itself, the objective arts of architecture and sculpture found in the marble quarries of Pentelicus, of Paros, and elsewhere a material which made many things possible which could not elsewhere have been attempted or imagined.

We understand what this means when we read that "the whole of the eastern side of Greece is formed of calcareous rock and crystalline schists, in which layer upon layer of the most superb marble is imbedded. Attica alone possesses three exquisite varieties—those of Pentelicus, Hymettus, and Laurium. Again, Bœotia, Laconia, and the Islands each has its own distinctive kind. Most striking of all is the island of Paros, which is simply a marble mountain, containing a supply so apparently endless as to lead to the fable among the ancients that its exhausted layers filled up again.

"Nor are these marbles all uniform in texture and appearance. Nature seems to have intended to train the artistic eye by offering for selection a choice the most varied. Sometimes the marble is of the purest, most dazzling whiteness, as is that of Paros; sometimes, after exposure in the air and polishing, it becomes of a faint golden hue, as in the marble of Pentelicus, seen in the temple of Theseus and in the ruins on the Acropolis of Athens. Or, again, the white background may be intersected by veins of color; blue, as in the marble of Hymettus; pale green, as in the Carystian marble of Eubœa; or yellow and gray, as in that of Laurium. . . .

"The Hellenes had the fine taste to avail themselves in their chief works exclusively of the pure varieties. They employed mainly the snowy white marble of Paros in their sculpture, the golden-tinged marble of Pentelicus in their architecture. The streaked and colored varieties were left for the bizarre taste of the Roman period."[26] The land furnished the material, but the Greeks molded the material into things of beauty to be a joy forever; for the Greeks were artistic in everything.

Matthew Arnold said that the Greek was an artist to his finger-tips, and that in the modern world the Japanese alone approached him in this respect; and Professor Lowes Dickinson, in his volume on *The Greek View of Life,* says: "The Greeks were by nature artists. They created works of art more purely beautiful than those of any other age or people. Their mere household crockery, their common pots and pans, were molded in shapes so ex-

---
[26]*Makers of Hellas,* pp. 40, 41.

quisitely graceful, and painted in designs so admirably drawn and composed, that any one of them has a higher artistic value than the whole contents of the British Royal Academy."[27] Professor Middleton is equally lavish in his praise. He declares, "The Greek workman was apparently incapable of making an ugly thing. Whatever the material he worked with, or whatever the object he wished to make, whether armor, personal ornament, or domestic vessels, the form was always especially adapted to its use, the ornament natural and graceful, so that the commonest water jar was a delight alike to him who made it and to him who used it."[28]

There are some wonderful little shoulder-pieces, called the "Siris bronzes," produced in the fourth century B. C., which are said to be the most exquisite bits of metal work in existence. Of them Professor Middleton writes, "No work of art in metal has probably ever surpassed these little figures for beauty, vigor, and expression, while the skill with which the artist has beaten these high reliefs out of a flat plate of metal appears almost miraculous."[29]

---

[27]Martin, *op. cit.*, p. 19.
[28]*Ibid.*, p. 19.
[29]*Ibid.*, p. 20.

THE GREEK TESTAMENT 45

There are series of Greek coins of which Mr. Ward says, "A small town, hardly heard of otherwise, will indicate by its coinage that it could command artists in that specialty such as the richest modern empires do not employ,"[30] and Mr. R. S. Poole, Keeper of the Coins and Metals Department of the British Museum, declares that "the excellence of the designs of very many Greek coins struck during the period of the best art is indeed so great that, were it not for their smallness, they would form the finest series of art studies in the world. . . . Every subject is ideal."[31]

A Greek house did not have many articles in it, but every article was a thing of beauty and represented the perfection of its kind. When they had reached perfection they were satisfied with it. Their styles did not change with each decade or each generation. Their ideals were retained for centuries. A vase was a family heirloom. A metal clasp, a hand mirror was a precious treasure to be handed down from father to son.

This love of art, cherished in the household, became characteristic of the race. Emil Reich, in his volume called *Success Among the Nations*, says, "Put their hands, put their

[30] Martin, *op. cit.*, p. 27.
[31] *Ibid.*, p. 27.

minds to what they would, the Greeks almost inevitably produced perfection,"[32] and when perfection once was produced they recognized it and reverenced it at its true worth. Pliny tells us that there was in Greece a picture so highly valued by the Greeks that the town which contained it was safe from attack. Demetrius would not assault the place where it was. We did not hear of any such reverence for art displayed by the combatant nations in the Great War in Europe. No one of those nations was artistic in everything. From this point of view they were brutal, savage, and degenerate alike.

It is true, as Professor Mahaffy has said, that "it is established beyond contradiction that the literary and artistic excellence of Greece before Alexander was never again attained by any nation or by any age." We all have been and are inferior to the Greeks of the Great Age. They attained perfection not only in the small articles we have mentioned—household utensils, vases, coins, and metal clasps—but in painting, sculpture, and architecture as well. Polygnotus was called the Homer of painting. Zeuxis the painter was considered the equal of Phidias the sculptor.

Apelles saw a picture upon which a would-be

---
[32]Martin, *op. cit.*, p. 59.

THE GREEK TESTAMENT 47

artist had labored for years and he said: "A great work! A great artist! It would be very famous—if there were but beauty in it!"[33] That painting has not survived, but that saying of Apelles survived as a statement of the first requirement of an enduring work of art, that it be beautiful. Apelles painted a portrait of Alexander and when that haughty youth saw it he did not praise it as it deserved to be praised. Then Alexander's horse was brought in and it neighed to the horse in the picture as if to a real one; and Apelles said to Alexander, "Sir, your horse appears to be a much better judge of painting than you are."[34]

A large number of funeral urns dating from 350 B. C. were found near Athens. One of them had a drawing of Aphrodite on a black swan. Of this picture Professor Middleton writes, "For delicacy of touch and refined beauty of drawing this painting is quite unrivaled. The exquisite loveliness of Aphrodite's head and the pure grace of her profile, touched in with simple, brush-formed lines, are quite indescribable, and show a combination of mechanical skill united to imaginative power and the realization of the most perfect and ideal beauty, such as no people but the

[33] Ælian, *Var. Hist.*, xii, 41.
[34] *Ibid.*, ii, 3.

Greeks have ever so completely possessed." The artist of this pottery painting is unknown, but his perfection of technique is simply an indication of the general if not universal excellence of work in this field in his day.

When we turn to architecture there can be only one verdict as to the Greek preeminence. Professor T. H. Lewis simply voices the unanimous opinion of those who are qualified to pronounce judgment when he says: "The Greeks have not been surpassed in the exquisite beauty of form and proportion, in the extreme simplicity and perfect harmony which pervade every part of their structures. . . . For all the higher effects which architecture is capable of producing, a Greek temple of the Doric order is perhaps unrivaled."[35]

We never consider Greek architecture without thinking of its consummate product in the Parthenon at Athens. It has been called "the supreme effort of genius in the pursuit of the beautiful." Of it Professor H. C. Butler, in his volume called *The Story of Athens,* has written: "There are no words in any language to describe the indefinable charm of the faultless completeness of the Parthenon. There is a finality about its perfect proportions which cannot be explained, but which leaves no doubt

---
[35]Martin, *op. cit.*, p. 15.

THE GREEK TESTAMENT 49

in the critic's mind that this is of all buildings the most flawless."[36]

We are more familiar with Greek sculpture than with any other form of Greek art, and here again the critics tell us that Greece is and ever will be supreme. Sturgis, in his work on *The Appreciation of Sculpture,* has said: "The best sculpture of the Greeks (479–350 B. C.) has been held to be more nearly faultless than any other class of works of fine art. This art, upon which all European arts of form have been based, remains the accepted model of all perfection. We do not know all that the Greek artist had in mind, but that which we have of his workmanship remains superior in pure form to aught which we find elsewhere."[37] Professor Mahaffy adds at this point: "The silver age of Greek art (which includes the Apollo Belvedere, the Laocoön, the Dying Gaul, the Venus of Melos, the sarcophagus of Sidon) was more splendid than the golden age of other nations."[38]

Let us not forget that while these masterpieces were the productions of individuals probably gifted above the common lot they

---

[36] Butler, *The Story of Athens,* p. 214. The Century Company. Used by permission.
[37] Martin, *op. cit.,* p. 14.
[38] *Ibid.,* p. 59.

were at the same time the culminations fostered by the universal appreciation of artistic perfection in everything, and that the general populace was artistic in its tastes and demands as no other people either before or since has been. One reason for this fact is to be found in the other fact that there was a higher average of intelligence and a more symmetrical type of education and a greater degree of general culture among the Greeks of the great century in their history than the world ever has seen elsewhere. The Greeks of that day came to believe with Aristotle that the difference between the educated and the uneducated was "the difference between the living and the dead."[39]

7. *Symmetrically Educated.* Professor West tells us that "The Greeks originated the idea of liberal education, meaning by this the training in selected studies of the most central character, so as to secure harmonious wholeness or integrity of intellectual culture. With that instinct for ideal unity and perfection which appears in everything they touched, they determined what ingredients should enter into their method and material of instruction by determining the ideal end of liberal educa-

---

[39] Diog. Laërt., v, 1. 19.

THE GREEK TESTAMENT 51

tion. There naturally grew up the idea of a logical sequence and coordination of studies to achieve this end—that is, of a curriculum." Real education thus became possible.

There were two controlling principles in both the theory and the practice in Greek education which after being neglected for centuries are now coming into their own again. Modern educators are beginning to acknowledge that the Greek philosophers were far in advance of all who have followed them in their insight into the proper methods to educate a people.

The first principle is that education must aim at the development of the individual, the drawing forth and making effective of all his latent powers and thus preparing him to render his personal and original contribution to the well-being of the state. It is not cramming his head full of facts. It is enlightening him as to his own privileges and responsibilities and powers. Plato said: "Education in the real sense is that education in virtue from youth upward, which makes a man eagerly pursue the ideal perfection of being a perfect citizen, and teaches him both how rightly to rule and how to obey. That is the only education which upon our view deserves the name. The other sort of training, which aims at mere cleverness apart from intelligence and justice, is mean and illiberal, and is not worthy to be called education at all."

The second principle is that of the harmonious development of all the faculties and powers. It is not the mind alone which needs to be educated but the tastes and the sensibilities, the moral and religious impulses; and the body is not to be neglected while the mind and soul are being trained, for the ideal product of the schools will be a man as perfect in physique as he is clear in his thinking and conscientious in his life.

What was the result of such training? The Greeks became "the most versatile and evenly developed race that nature has yet brought forth." They had great powers which they kept in equipoise. As Maurice Croiset has expressed it: "The Hellene always possessed judgment in imagination, intellect in sentiment, and reflection in passion. We never see him entirely carried away in one direction." The Greeks thought deeply and saw clearly and therefore were orderly and symmetrical in all their creations. Their temples and their epics, their statues and their states were not lop-sided and extravagant, but every detail was made to subserve the interest and beauty of the whole. Their sense of proportion saved

THE GREEK TESTAMENT 53

them from excess and the ugliness of overemphasis in anything.

Their motto was μηδὲν ἄγαν, "Nothing in excess." Their favorite virtues were αἰδώς and σωφροσύνη, modesty and self- restraint. Reverence and soberness characterized their conduct and their work. They despised eccentricity. They aspired to completeness, rounded and symmetrical; but they found their ideal of beauty in brevity and simplicity and moderation rather than in any extravagance. Among their proverbs were these, "The half is greater than the whole," and "Sow with the hand and not with the whole sack."

Plato arranged and rearranged the first eight words of the Republic, and that work when completed was a comparatively small book, but it has influenced philosophical thought more than any of the massive tomes since published in that field. The whole of Thucydides could be printed in any average-sized modern city newspaper, and would anybody doubt that Thucydides is worth more to the world with all his terseness and brevity than a million modern newspapers with their pages on pages of advertisements and comics and superfluous and questionable news? The Greeks aimed at truth and beauty as well as perfection in form, and they found all of these in simplicity of expression in both literature and art. They ignored the accidental. They had no time for the insignificant. They instinctively turned away from the ugly. They gave themselves to the typical and salient and beautiful and permanent, and they remain the artistic and intellectual masters of the world to-day.

8. *Highest in Culture.* We know the result of this education and aspiration upon the Greek race. Galton claims that the average ability of the Athenian race was about as much above ours as ours is above that of the African Negro. Darwin, in *The Descent of Man,* declares "that the old Greeks stood some grades higher in intellect than any race that has ever existed,"[40] and we must remember that that statement applies not to the upper classes of Greek society alone but to the middle and lower classes as well. It was this fact which impressed Matthew Arnold so deeply, the spectacle of the middle and the lower classes in the highest development of their humanity that these classes have ever yet reached; and he declared that was why a handful of Athenians of two thousand years ago are more interesting than the millions of our contemporaries.

---

[40] Darwin, *Descent of Man,* p. 156. D. Appleton & Co. Used by permission.

THE GREEK TESTAMENT 55

John Stuart Mill in his volume on Representative Government includes other elements than the schools in the production of the result but he agrees that there was a higher average of intelligence in Greece than in any other country. He says, "The practice of the dicastery and the ecclesia at Athens raised the intellectual standard of the average citizen far beyond anything of which there is yet an example in any other mass of men, ancient or modern."[41] Professor Greene, of Harvard, states his conclusion as follows: "During the fifty years between the Persian wars and the great Peloponnesian War the men of Athens, whose citizenship was carefully restricted, developed a type of average citizen whose political experience and sagacity, whose contact with life in varied occupations, and whose capacity for appreciating beauty and reason has been surpassed by the average of no other race or time."[42] Sir Robert Collier declared, "An Athenian jury was probably more intelligent than any popular assembly which has ever existed before or since."

Freeman rather audaciously asserts that the intelligence of an Athenian audience, assem-

---

[41]Mill, *Representative Government*, p. 78. Longmans, Green and Company. Used by permission.

[42]Greene, *The Achievement of Greece*, p. 45.

bled to hear a new play of Sophocles or Æschylus, was higher than that of the present House of Commons, although the first consisted of the ordinary citizens, while the second was made up of picked men.[43] Arthur Elam Haigh has written a volume on The Attic Theater and in it he says, "As far as intelligence and discrimination are concerned, the Athenian audiences were probably superior to any audience of the same size which has ever been brought together."

This, then, according to the best authorities, was the result of this symmetrical education among the Greeks of the Great Age, that they attained a higher degree of culture than the world has seen before or since. Lübke, in his *History of Art,* declares, "The Greeks reached an absolute height of culture. Their whole mental life was so elevated, so filled with universal human significance that it furnishes a basis for the culture of all future ages."[44] John Fiske agrees in the conclusion that "of no other community have the members been so highly cultivated. It was not merely literary culture which they possessed, but that sort which is derived from direct intercourse

---

[43]Freeman, *History of Federal Government*, vol. i, p. 37sqq.

[44]Martin, *op. cit.*, pp. 60, 61.

THE GREEK TESTAMENT 57

with nature and life and constant familiarity with the thoughts of rich and powerful minds."[45]

They had no aristocracy at Athens, either of blood or of wealth. The only aristocracy they recognized was an aristocracy of intellect. John Henry Newman says that in Athens "there was no sovereignty but that of mind, and no nobility but that of genius, where professors were rulers and princes did homage." When Dionysius the Tyrant aspired to be a poet, Philoxenus expressed great contempt for his verses, and Dionysius sent him to the stone quarries for punishment. Later he was released and invited again to hear Dionysius read his poems. After listening for a time Philoxenus rose to go. "Whither now?" asked Dionysius. "To the quarries," said Philoxenus. He was no flatterer of a tyrant. He would praise nothing but genius. He would tell the truth and go to jail for it.

The Greeks had faith that Truth was man's friend and that Truth was accessible to any man. They honored most highly the men who could lead them into new truth of any kind. They had no kings or lords or barons or nobles. They had no bishops, no pretentious or established hierarchy. They had no million-

---
[45]Martin, *op. cit.*, pp. 60, 61.

aires, no trusts, no monopolies, no giant combinations in restraint of trade. They had no tramps and no paupers. They had moderate comforts, artistic utensils, general intelligence, good health, and the highest degree of culture any community of men ever has enjoyed.

In Egypt and Babylonia what science they had was in the hands of the priests and soon became involved in religious ritual and then degenerated into lifeless formulæ. There was no organized priesthood among the Greeks, and they could give their reasoning faculties free play without any repressing influence from that source. There were no dogmas to lay chill hands upon original thought. There were no superstitions or traditions so sacred as to be unquestioned or to preclude any progress in truth.

No interlocking directorates of financial magnates or ecclesiastical obscurantists hindered the freedom of investigation and the advancement of learning in any line. Any Greek could create a science capable of limitless development. All Greeks were free to think for themselves and to cooperate for the common good. G. K. Chesterton speaks of "the beautiful and astonishing pagan world" and then says of it, "It was a world in which common sense was really common."[46] Our modern world knows many things which the Greeks did not know; but it seems to know far less than they about the art of living healthfully, happily, and usefully.

The Greeks had a democracy which aimed at the welfare of the whole population and which attained that ideal in a higher measure than any other people of either ancient or modern times. When Solon was asked how wrongdoing can be avoided in a state he answered, "If those who are not wronged feel the same indignation at it as those who are."[47] Mutual sympathy and cooperation in common repudiation of any unrighteousness would insure and maintain the perfect state. In the pursuit of that ideal the Greek democracies became the models of all after time. It remains to say that in their Great Age the Greeks were more prolific in genius than any other race has been.

9. *Prolific in Genius.* John Fiske asserts that "Athens produced a larger number of men of the highest caliber than any other community which has ever existed." Professor Mahaffy says, "The great fact about the

---
[46]Cooper, *The Greek Genius and Its Influence*, p. 273. Yale University Press. Used by permission.

[47]Stobæus, *Flor.* xliii, 77.

Greeks is the extraordinary frequency of exceptional genius among them," and then he adds: "This is the greatest claim which any nation can bring to the admiration of posterity."[48] Lecky declares, "It is one of the anomalies of history that within the narrow limits and scanty populace of Greece arose men who in almost every form of genius, philosophy, epic, dramatic, and lyric poetry, eloquence, statesmanship, sculpture, painting, probably also in music, attained almost or altogether the highest limits of human perfection."[49]

We are told that the little city of Athens produced in a few years more men of consummate genius than did all the millions of inhabitants of China, Arabia, India, Palestine, Rome, Carthage, and all of Europe for two thousand years, and that in the production of genius Greece is still equal to Rome, Italy, Palestine, America, England, and Germany all counted together.[50] Professor E. A. Freeman believes that "the one century of Athenian greatness, from the expulsion of the tyrants to the defeat of Ægos Potamos, is worth mil-

---

[48] Martin, *op. cit.*, p. 60.
[49] Lecky, *History of European Morals*, vol. 1, p. 418. D. Appleton & Co. Used by permission.
[50] Martin, *op. cit.*, pp. 49-50.

THE GREEK TESTAMENT 61

lenniums of the life of Egypt or Assyria." Withington says, "In the age of Pericles there lived within the narrow limits of the Greek world more men of genius than ever existed together since."[51]

Can we get a better conception of this wealth of all that makes a nation great through a concrete illustration? "On a certain afternoon about 469 B. C. there was assembled at the theater in Athens a concourse of citizens to witness a dramatic contest. Among those present were Æschylus, Sophocles, Euripides, Cimon, Anaxagoras, Pericles, Thucydides, and Phidias. That is to say, the greatest tragedy-writer, the greatest statesman, the greatest historian, and the greatest artist of all time, with a great philosopher and a host of other artists and poets whose fame has lasted through twenty centuries."[52]

In one family of four generations in Athens the acquaintance could have included Æschylus, Sophocles, Euripides, Pericles, Socrates, Anaxagoras, Aristophanes, Thucydides, Themistocles, Herodotus, Polygnotus, Ictinus, Leonidas, Cimon, Epaminondas, Phocion, Pythagoras, Plato, Aristotle, Xenophon, Æschines, Praxiteles, Demosthenes, Anacreon, Pindar,

[51]Martin, op. cit., p. 57.
[52]Ibid., pp. 57-58.

Apelles, Euclid, and Hippocrates. We stop with these names; but there are others worthy of a place in this galaxy of stars, this constellation of genius unsurpassed in any clime or at any time. With such general intelligence and such an accumulation of genius unprecedented and unparalleled in any other period and place in world history we are not surprised that Lecky should tell us that in almost every form of human endeavor the Greeks "attained almost or altogether the highest limits of human perfection."[53]

10. *Incomparable in Achievement.* "What have they not done? Supreme in poetry and prose, in architecture and sculpture, in painting and music, in grammar, logic, mathematics, and medicine, in politics, sociology, and law, in philosophy and theology, they are also supreme in science; for, though they did not discover the powers of steam or electricity, they nevertheless carried out in mechanics works that no modern builder, with all his vaunted control of nature, has yet equaled."[54]

Henry Cabot Lodge speaks of the wonderful achievements of applied science in our day, of the steam engine and the telegraph, the telephone, the dynamo and the motor car, wireless

---
[53] Lecky, *History of European Morals*, vol. i, p. 418.
[54] Hastings, *Expository Times*, vol. xxi, p. 184.

THE GREEK TESTAMENT 63

telegraphy and aeroplanes and he also mentions the submarine, the poisonous gas, the high explosives, and all the new devices for the sudden obliteration of human lives, and then he adds: "The spirit of man, that which is highest in him, is not lifted up and strengthened by an automobile, or a traction engine, or even by an incandescent electric lamp. But the thoughts of men, of the philosophers, the moralists and the preachers of religion, of artists and architects, of the dramatists, the singers and the poets, whether conveyed to us in paintings, statues and buildings, or in books, are the real forces which have moved the world."[55]

It is here that the Greeks excelled. Mill said of them, "The Greeks are the most remarkable people who have ever existed. . . . They were the beginners of nearly everything, Christianity excepted, of which the modern world makes its boast. . . . They were the founders of mathematics, of physics, of the inductive study of politics, of the philosophy of human nature and life. In each they made the indispensable first steps, which are the foundation of all the rest."[56]

---

[55]West, *The Value of the Classics*, p. 119. Princeton University Press. Used by permission.

[56]Mill, *Dissertations*, vol. ii, p. 283f. E. P. Dutton & Co. Used by permission.

When Anaxagoras was asked for what purpose he was born, his answer was, "To contemplate the works of nature." The Greeks saw things as they really were and asked and ascertained the reasons for the things they saw. They came to be the "great masters of those who know," the great teachers of all Europe and America in science and philosophy, in literature and art, the models of all who have come after them in saying and thinking and doing the really good and truly great. Richly endowed with mental gifts, incomparably fertile in the most invaluable products of civilization and culture, inexhaustibly rich in thought and thought-expression, Greece has been to the centuries the ideal of literary and artistic excellence, the object of the world's wonder and admiration, enthusiastic study and love. It remains unsurpassed to-day.

The Greeks aimed at absolute perfection both of the human form and of the human intellect and came nearer to the realization of both ideals than any other people ever did. There were intellectual giants in those days, the great old giants who wrestled with the ultimate secrets in the heart of nature and in the mind of man, and who put the products of their research and their thought into such perfect and imperishable form that the scholar-

THE GREEK TESTAMENT 65

ship of the world to-day looks back to them still for its substance and its inspiration.

The Greeks had the best epics, the best dramas, the best orations, the highest grades of literature, the ideal temples and altars and shrines; in Dorian simplicity, Ionian magnificence, and Attic perfection of detail, the highest forms of art-expression the world ever has seen. Among the mighty nations of antiquity the Greeks stood first. Always "politically weak, numerically small, materially poor," they were the chosen of God to develop the intellect to its highest and best. Their little land, so insignificant in size, the smallest of the three southern peninsulas of Europe, cramped between its many mountains, hemmed in and almost swept across by sea, seemed crowded full to suffocation with thinkers, writers, statesmen of the first degree. It became the home of genius, the source of culture, the acknowledged birth-land of the intellectual life of the modern world.

The land was a wonderful land. Its people was a wonderful people. They are both worth our knowing and knowing well.

PART III

A WONDERFUL LANGUAGE

LANGUAGES differ radically among themselves; but while each of the modern nations is proud of its mother-tongue and will dispute its supremacy with any of its contemporaries, the scholars and competent authorities of the world are completely agreed in conceding that the classical Greek is in many ways superior to all of its successors and the well-nigh perfect medium for the utterances of genius and the expression of thought. The Greek language is a remarkable one in many respects and possibly the most noteworthy product of the Greek nation. That would be high praise indeed, for the Greeks gave us the Iliad and the Parthenon; but their first creation and their most valuable legacy was their own Greek tongue.

Professor Felton declares, "The Greek language is the most flexible and transparent body in which human thought has ever been clothed." Farrar agrees when he says, "The Aryan family of languages is the most perfect

THE GREEK TESTAMENT 67

family in the world, and Greek is the most perfect language in this family; it is the instinctive metaphysics of the most intelligent of nations."[1] The historian Grote adds his testimony, "The Hellenic language is the noblest among the many varieties of human speech."[2]

Henry Nelson Coleridge says about this language: "Greek is the shrine of the genius of the Old World; as universal as our race, as individual as ourselves; of infinite flexibility, of indefatigable strength, with the complication and the distinctness of Nature herself: to which nothing was vulgar, from which nothing was excluded; speaking to the ear like Italian, speaking to the mind like English; with words like pictures, with words like the gossamer film of the summer; uniting at once the variety and picturesqueness of Homer with the gloom and intensity of Æschylus. It is not compressed to the closest by Thucydides, not fathomed to the bottom by Plato, not sounding with all its thunders, nor lit up with all its ardors, even under the Promethean touch of Demosthenes."[3]

---

[1] Farrar, *Greek Syntax*, p. 1. Longmans, Green & Company. Used by permission.
[2] Martin, *op. cit.*, p. 43.
[3] Coleridge, *Introduction to the Study of the Greek Classic Poets.*

It is a marvelous language, "made," as Professor Harris has said, "for all that is great and all that is beautiful, in every subject, and under every form of writing." "The Greeks excelled in an instinct for beauty and in the power of creating beautiful forms: and, of all the beautiful things which they created, their own language was the first and the most wonderful"; a language which in meter and music, in richness and variety, in fertility of flection and delicacy of intricate expression, in flexibility and multiform capacity, in sweetness and strength was and is unrivaled among the many tongues of the world. The ancient Sanscrit lacks its smoothness and infinite freedom of vowel sounds; modern French has no hint of its strength and anomalous use of primary and indispensable root-forms. The makers of such a language were of necessity the masters of expression in every phase of thought.

Poetry is the test of any language's beauty, flexibility, and strength; and we may well agree with Principal Shairp when he writes, "Didactic, lyric, tragic, comic poetry—each of these in Greece first came to light, and there too found its consummate form."[4] Look at the

---
[4]Shairp, *Culture and Religion*, p. 36. Houghton Mifflin Company. Used by permission.

THE GREEK TESTAMENT 69

great names, from Homer, "the first Apostle of Civilization," as Doctor Newman has called him, to Aristophanes, the prince of the Old Comedy; Hesiod, Pindar, Æschylus, Sophocles, Euripides, Anacreon, and Sappho; crowned by universal verdict the unapproachable masters, each in his special line. All later poets derive from them.

The Greeks did the hard thinking for all the Western lands. Their language has set its seal on all the arts and sciences. The technical terminology of these, and the very names by which they are to be known to all time, the Greeks have given them. When we speak of architecture and astronomy and anthropology and physiology and psychology and physics and biology and zoology and pathology and ethnology and philology and epistemology and music and mathematics and philosophy and geography and geology and geometry and economics and rhetoric and logic and botany and anatomy and arithmetic and history and poetry and politics and theology we are using Greek words to name departments of learning which the Greeks first developed into perfect form. When we speak of athletics and mechanics and the epic and the lyric and the drama and democracy and autocracy and aristocracy and oligarchy we are using Greek words in the sense in which the Greeks first used them.

Philosophy is a Greek word and all philosophy is Greek. Unless we make the word so indefinite in meaning as to empty it of all special content, we may say that there never has been any modern philosophy which could not be traced to Greek influences. The realistic and idealistic philosophers of to-day fight over the problems set forth by Plato and Aristotle, and add little or nothing to the conclusions arrived at by these great masters in this field. Historians now are either pictorial or philosophical and follow after either Herodotus or Thucydides. The orations of Demosthenes and Pericles stand preeminent for all time, the Greek race, climate, and customs furnishing the conditions for the perfect development of oratory such as no other country ever will be able to produce.

The motto written over the Academy was μηδεὶς ἀγεωμέτρητος εἰσίτω, "Let no one enter here who is without a knowledge of geometry." Dionysius, the Tyrant of Syracuse, whom we have mentioned before, sent for Plato to help him build a model state, but when he found that Plato considered a sound knowledge of mathematics the first requisite for any student of statecraft his enthusiasm began to wane

THE GREEK TESTAMENT 71

at once. The typical Greek loved mathematics, was attracted by the marvels of number and fascinated by the laws of order and harmony and measurement. The Greeks were the first mathematicians. The technical equipment of pure geometry is almost wholly Greek.

Euclid was a typical Greek. He wrote a textbook on the elements of geometry in the fourth or the third century B. C. which was in practically continuous use in the schools up to the present century. It is very seldom that a scientific textbook lasts longer than a single generation; but Euclid was a textbook for more than two thousand years. The principles and terminology of that textbook were so accurate and sufficient that they have remained unchanged through the centuries. It is doubtful whether any book except the Bible has had such an uninterrupted vogue.

Its terms are the terms used to-day. The isosceles triangle is a triangle with equal legs, the compound term being made up of the two elements, ἴσυς and σκέλος, recognizable at once by the Greek student but apt to be a puzzle to anyone ignorant of the language which gave it the name. Parallel lines are those which go alongside one another all the way, παρ ἀλλήλας. A parallelogram is a figure contained within parallel lines, παράλληλος and γραμμή.

72 GREEK CULTURE AND

A parallelepiped is a solid figure bounded by three pairs of parallel planes, παράλληλος and ἐπίπεδος, a plane. Euclid wrote of ἡ τὴν ὀρθὴν γωνίαν ὑποτείνουσα πλευρά, the side subtending the right-angle, and that feminine participle, hypotenuse, has been used ever since as a name for that side of the right-angled triangle. These terms are apt to seem outlandish and unaccountable to the schoolboy with no knowledge of Greek. They are perfectly simple and clear to the one who has command of the language which created them; and whether we understand them or not, we all use them and will continue to use them in all coming time.

Huxley stated our debt to the Greeks when he said: "The foundations of mathematics were so well laid by them, that our children learn their geometry from a book written for the schools of Alexandria more than two thousand years ago. Modern astronomy is the natural continuation and development of the works of Hipparchus and Ptolemy; modern physics of that of Democritus and Archimedes; it was long before modern biological science outgrew the knowledge bequeathed to us by Aristotle, by Theophrastus, and by Galen."[5] What Cicero said of his day is

---

[5]Huxley, *Science and Culture*, p. 16. D. Appleton & Co. Used by permission.

THE GREEK TESTAMENT 73

equally true of our own, "In learning and in every branch of literature, the Greeks are our masters."[6]

The poet Shelley paid his tribute to this wonderful tongue, "Their very language . . . in variety, in simplicity, in flexibility, and in copiousness, excels every other language of the Western world," and then he acknowledged our debt to the race in these words, "We are all Greeks. Our laws, our literature, our religion, our arts, have their root in Greece. The human form and the human mind attained to a perfection in Greece which has impressed its image on those faultless productions whose very fragments are the despair of modern art, and has propagated impulses which cannot cease, through a thousand channels of manifest or imperceptible operation, to ennoble and delight mankind until the extinction of the race."[7]

> "Her citizens, imperial spirits,
> Rule the present from the past;
> On all this world of man inherits
> Their seal is set."[8]

"Our roots are so entwined in the soil of

---
[6] Cicero, *Tusc.* iii, 1. 2.
[7] Shelley, Preface to Hellas, Oxford edition, *Shelley's Poetical Works*, p. 442.
[8] *Ibid.*, p. 464.

Greek culture that we can never lose the taste of it as long as books are read and pictures painted. We are, in fact, living on the legacy of Greece." Most of us do not realize this fact as fully as we might. Livingstone has illustrated it in one department of our modern life in this graphic manner. A man walking down the city street "passes the *Lyric Theater*. If it is the evening, a *dramatic* performance is probably taking place inside. It may be a *tragedy*, or some form of *comedy*. If it is a *musical comedy* and he enters, he will see elaborate *scenery* and a play which may open with a *prologue* and which is partly composed of *dialogue* between the various *characters*, partly of songs in various *meters*, sung by a *chorus* to the accompaniment of an *orchestra*. As the words in italics indicate, our imaginary passer-by will have seen, though he may not have suspected it, a symbol of the indelible mark which the Greeks have set on the æsthetic and intellectual life of Europe, and of the living presence of Greece in the twentieth century."[9]

Goethe said: "Study Molière, study Shakespeare, but before all study the ancient Greeks —always the Greeks." It has been suggested

---
[9] Livingstone, *The Pageant of Greece*, p. 1. The Clarendon Press, Oxford. Used by permission.

THE GREEK TESTAMENT 75

that learning a new language is like entering a new world. Surely no other language is the open gate to so wonderful a world of culture and literature as this language of the Greeks in which " 'the blind old bard of Scio's rocky isle' entranced all the listening generations, and the great trio of tragedians educated Athens, and the Stagirite philosopher hewed out the channels in which human reasoning will ever flow, and the most illustrious pupil of Socrates uttered his 'divine peradventures,' and the unconquerable king of the bema swayed at will the fierce democracy of Athens."

This language is indisputably "the most effective instrument for the discipline of the imagination, taste, and expression" which the human intellect, unaided, has produced. As Professor Ladd declares, "No other ancient language possessed anything like the same capacity for figurative construction, the same manifoldness, versatility, and wealth of words and ideas." It was the medium through which the highest efforts of human genius found their way into world literature and world life. Therefore the Greek language has become an essential element in all world progress. It is what Bishop Alexander said of it, "the musical and 'golden tongue which gave a soul to the objects of sense and a body to the abstractions of philosophy'; the language of a people whose mission it was to give a principle of fermentation to all races of mankind, susceptible to those subtle and largely indefinable influences which are called collectively Progress."[10]

Therefore, it was capable of keeping pace with the advancing thought of the centuries. It passed from pagan into Christian use, and was just as serviceable in the latter as it had been in the former. It had the metaphysics of time in its tenses and the metaphysics of space in its cases and it was capable of immortal life.

In her account of the Greek Christian poets Elizabeth Barrett Browning has said of the Greek language, "Blind Homer spoke this Greek after blind Demodocus, with a quenchless light about his brows, which he felt through his blindness. Pindar rolled his chariots in it, prolonging the clamor of the games. Sappho's heart beat through it, and heaved up the world's. Æschylus strained it to the stature of his high thoughts. Plato crowned it with his divine peradventures. Aristophanes made it drunk with the wine of his fantastic merriment. The later Platon-

---

[10] Alexander, *The Epistles of John*, pp. 104-105. George H. Doran Company. Used by permission.

THE GREEK TESTAMENT 77

ists wove their souls away in it, out of sight of other souls. The first Christians heard in it God's new revelation, and confessed their Christ in it from the suppliant's knee and presently from the bishop's throne. To all times, and their transitions, the language lent itself through a long summer of above two thousand years."[11]

Strangely vital was this wonderful language of the Greeks. It seemed as if mankind could not consent to part with it, and no progressive race ever will be able to part with it. It has linked itself indissolubly to all intellectual endeavor. It contains not only the invaluable treasures of the past but also the indispensable potencies of all progress in the future days. It is all that Ammi B. Hyde has said of it, "Compared with the Sanscrit, its stationary sister, or the Latin, older but unmanipulated, the Greek issues from demiurgic darkness into historic day, a 'crystalline delight,' complete in every linguistic quality, tuneful now as ever beneath its sapphire skies, fit for gods and godlike men."[12]

A modern traveler reminds us that "it is nonsense to treat Greek as if it were a dead language. It is living in the speech, journal-

[11] Mrs. Browning, *Letters and Essays*, vol. ii, p. 120.
[12] Methodist Review, 1897, p. 222.

ism, and literature of the Greeks to-day. . . . The letters, the accents are the same. The old Greek has changed its form in modern usage. It is simpler, less accurate, less rich in moods and inflections, but it is historically, essentially the same language. One may open his Homer and pick out on every page words that are in common usage to-day, after three thousand years of currency. The universal daily greeting, χαίρετε, is Homeric. The resemblance to the New Testament Greek is remarkable."[13] The Greek lives to-day. We shall have more to say upon that point later.

In the beginning there were three clearly defined dialects in the Greek. First, the Ionic, used in ancient Attica and its colonies in Asia Minor and elsewhere. It was the tongue of Homer, Hesiod, and Herodotus. It always remained the favorite form of the language for epic poetry. Second, the Æolic, used in Thessaly, Bœotia, and some colonies of Asia Minor. It was the dialect of Sappho and Alcæus. Third, the Doric, used in the Peloponnesus and in the Doric colonies. It was the language of Pindar; and remained the favorite form for lyric poetry in war songs, religious hymns, and the choruses. Later, and supplanting all of these, came the Attic Greek.

---

[13]Barrows, *The Isles and Shrines of Greece.*

THE GREEK TESTAMENT 79

It was the language developed to its perfect form at Athens, the center of Greek culture, when that culture had arrived at its fullest and richest growth. Most of the great authors in Greek literature used this tongue: Plato, Aristotle, Thucydides, Xenophon, Æschylus, Sophocles, Euripides, Aristophanes, and Demosthenes. As these names will indicate, the Attic writers excel in the drama, in oratory, in history, and in philosophy. Attic Greek, recognized as the finest form the language had attained, came to be the common written language of the Greeks everywhere.

In the course of time, transplanted to many foreign lands and incorporating many foreign elements, it became in a measure degenerate and was rechristened and called the Common or Hellenic Greek. This is represented in literature by Plutarch and Plotinus and the later Greek writers and finally found its best-known literary monument in the New Testament of the Christian Church. It was customary to call the New Testament Greek biblical Greek or Judæan Greek or Hellenistic Greek, and to say that it was distinguished from the Hellenic Greek by the Hebraisms and the Aramaic idioms found in it.

In 1894 Friedrich Blass said that New Testament Greek was "to be recognized as something peculiar, obeying its own laws." In 1889 Edwin Hatch wrote, "Biblical Greek is thus a language which stands by itself."[14] In 1883 Cremer adopted the words of Richard Rothe and declared, "We can indeed with good right speak of a language of the Holy Ghost. For in the Bible it is manifest to our eyes how the Divine Spirit at work in revelation always takes the language of a particular people chosen to be the recipient and makes of it a characteristic religious variety by transforming existing linguistic elements and existing conceptions into a shape peculiarly appropriate to that Spirit. This process is shown most clearly by the Greek of the New Testament."

That was the way the scholars talked a generation or two ago, but "the language of the Holy Ghost" is not now considered so peculiar as it once was. Within the last generation there have been numerous finds of Greek papyri which have brought us into much closer touch with the ordinary speech of the people in the New Testament times than we ever have been before; and one of the first things which has been made clear is that the old-time distinction between Hellenistic and Hellenic Greek no longer can be held valid.

---

[14]Hatch, *Essays in Biblical Greek*, p. 11. The Clarendon Press, Oxford. Used by permission.

THE GREEK TESTAMENT 81

Almost all of the "Hebraisms" of our grammars and commentaries and lexicons have been found in the Greek current in Egypt, Asia Minor, and even in Greece itself, where there is no reason to suppose any Semitic influence whatever. In the light furnished by Deissmann and Milligan and Moulton and other workers upon the new material now first open to us in these papyri finds, we will need to revise all our authorities at these points. The New Testament was written in the current or Common Greek; and it looks more and more as if not only Paul but the other New Testament writers as well, and if they then in all probability their Master, Jesus, were bilingual and had been acquainted with the current Greek language and idioms from their childhood days.

However that may be, it is increasingly evident that the newly coined words in the New Testament are decreasing in number with the new discoveries of every day. Whereas we used to think that about twelve per cent of the words in the New Testament were peculiar to its Hellenistic Greek, we know now that not more than one per cent, not more than fifty out of the five thousand words in the vocabulary of the New Testament, can be so regarded; and this number may diminish with further finds of contemporary documents in the neighboring lands. "The language of the Holy Ghost" in our New Testament turns out to be the language of the common folk in all the world of that time, since for the first time in world history there was a world language.

It is no exaggeration to say that this Greek of the common speech had become a world language, for the inscriptions and the papyri prove its presence and its prevalence not only in Greece but in Rome and Marseilles and Carthage and Cyrene and Sicily and Egypt and Asia Minor and all parts of the world empire. There was an international language in the days of the Christ. The babel of tongues had been supplanted by the best of the ancient forms of speech. In the whole of the Diaspora, says Schurer, "Greek was the mother tongue of the Jews. All the relics of writing that have come down to us from the Diaspora during the last centuries B. C. and the first centuries A. D. are in Greek."[15]

It is not strange therefore that the Epistle to the Hebrews was written in Greek and that Paul wrote to the church at Rome in Greek, for both the Jews and the Romans spoke Greek. The Roman Emperor Marcus Aurelius

---

[15]Hastings' *Dictionary of the Bible*, vol. v, p. 108. Charles Scribner's Sons. Used by permission.

THE GREEK TESTAMENT 83

wrote his *Meditations* in Greek. The whole of the New Testament was written in Greek, and Christianity through its literature and its missionary propaganda helped much to maintain and to spread the supremacy of the Greek tongue. Sir William Ramsay declares that it was Christianity alone which led to the final triumph of the Greek speech over the many native dialects of Asia Minor.

The New Testament Greek had beauties of its own. It was rude and commonplace in comparison with the perfections of the classical Greek, but it had a directness and a simplicity and a power peculiar to itself. The parable of the prodigal son has gripped the attention and the conscience of the world as surely as any of the great passages in the ancient Greek literature. Its literary excellences are apparent to all who read. It is only an example of the union of the Hebrew religious spirit with the precision of the Greek expression to be found in the entire New Testament. The directness and the vitality of Hebrew thought finds fitting and adequate form in the delicacies of the Greek grammatical inflexions.

As the language of the common people everywhere the New Testament Greek is better fitted than the classical Greek would have been to convey the Hebrew truth to the world.

It has a vitality of its own which Joseph Henry Thayer says "resides in the spirit which quickens it. This discloses itself on every page. It ushers a reader into a new realm of thought, and introduces him to a new type of life. . . . It is as pervasive as the atmosphere, but as intangible as a perfume."[16] The vitality of the language is an aid to the revelation and the vitality of the revelation is an assurance of the immortality of the language in which it is enshrined.

We recognize the three primitive dialects of the Greek, the Ionic, the Æolic, and the Doric, and following them the consummate form in the Attic, and following this the universal form in the Common or Hellenic Greek. In these latter forms all that Professor Briggs says of this language is true of it. "The Greek is the beautiful flower, the elegant jewel, the most finished masterpiece of Indo-Germanic thought. In its early beginning we see a number of dialects spoken by a brave and warlike people, struggling with one another as well as with external foes, maintaining themselves successfully against the Oriental and African civilizations, while at the same time they appropriated those elements of culture which they could incorporate into their own original

---

[16]Hastings' *Dictionary of the Bible*, vol. iii, p. 40.

THE GREEK TESTAMENT 85

thought and life; a race of heroes such as the earth has nowhere else produced, fighting their way upward into light and culture until they attained the towering summits of an art, a literature, and a philosophy that has ever been the admiration and wonder of mankind. . . .

"The Greek was a thorough artist; and as the palaces of his princes, the temples of his gods, the images of his worship, his clothing and his armor, must be perfect in form and exquisite in finished decoration, so the language, as the palace, the dress of his thought, must be symmetrical and elegant. Hence there is no language that has such laws of euphony, involving changes in vocalization, and the transposition and mutation of letters; for their words must be musical, their clauses harmonious, their sentences and periods symmetrical. And so they are combined in the most exquisite taste in the dialogues of the philosopher, the measures of the poet, the stately periods of the historian and the orator."[17]

This language, once formed, found its way into recognition and supremacy everywhere. It became the intellectual bond of the civilized world. At the beginning of the Christian era

---
[17]Briggs, *The Study of Holy Scripture*, pp. 64–66. Charles Scribner's Sons. Used by permission.

it was the prevalent language in the commercial and the literary life of all the lands. This is evident from the testimony of the writers of that day. Cicero, in his Oration for the poet Archias, 68 B. C., said, "For if anyone suppose that less fame is derived from verses written in Greek than from those in Latin, he is greatly mistaken; because Greek literature is read in nearly all nations—Latin literature is confined within its own limits, certainly narrow, Quod Græca leguntur in omnibus fere gentibus, Latina suis finibus, exiguis sane, continentur." Quintillian maintains that all Roman boys should study Greek, "because Latin learning is derived from Greek."[18] Juvenal, who was contemporary with the apostles, in his Sixth Satire bewails the fact that Greek is in full possession of the world. "Everything is done in Greek," he says. "In this language they fear; in this they pour forth their wrath, their joys, their sorrows: in this, all the secrets of their breasts. Omnia Græca. Hoc sermone pavent, hoc iram, gaudia, causas, hoc cuncta affundunt, animi secreta."

The reasons for this prevalence of the Greek tongue are easily seen.

1. As we already have stated, the Greeks were the colonizers of the ancient world. They

---
[18]Quintillian, *Inst. Or.* I, i, 12.

founded cities and colonies in Italy, Gaul, Asia Minor, and all about the Ægean and the Black Seas; and wherever they went they carried their language with them. They clearly recognized the intellectual superiority of their own nation, and in the midst of the barbarians everywhere they preserved their native tongue and maintained their national characteristics.

2. Alexander the Great was a world conqueror, and he was the greatest of the world conquerors because he not only conquered the world but he colonized it and civilized it as well. He established the Greek arts and customs and language wherever his conquering armies came. He did many great and good things, but surely this deserves to rank among his greatest achievements, that he gave a common tongue, and such a tongue, to the civilized world.

3. Introduced by the roving disposition and the maritime habits of the Greek nation, and established by the world conquest of Alexander the Great, the ascendancy of the Greek tongue was maintained by the world-wide acknowledgment of the unrivaled supremacy of the Greek culture, the invaluable treasures of the Greek literature, and the beauty and power of the Greek language itself.

Thus it came to pass that everybody knew

the Greek language in the time of our Lord. All the first Christians spoke Greek, and for some centuries all the Christians who wrote books wrote them in Greek and in nothing but Greek. The church spread rapidly through the limits of the Roman Empire, and the apostles and the early Church Fathers lived and labored in Asia, in Africa, in Europe; but whether it appeared in the East or the West, the North or the South, all the Christian literature of the first centuries of Christianity's life and growth was Greek and only Greek. The Gospels, the Acts, the Epistles, the Apocalypses, the Apologies, the Commentaries, the Theologies were all Greek. Anybody who would understand this first period in church history and would get at the original sources must know Greek. Any specialist in theology, any student of the beginnings of Christianity, any preacher or expounder of God's Word, and, as it would seem, any earnest Christian surely would think it worth while to become thoroughly familiar with the Greek.

Is it worth while for anybody else to study Greek? We live in a practical age, and most people think they have no time for things which are of little or no practical benefit. Many people have made money and achieved social position and endowed universities who

THE GREEK TESTAMENT 89

knew nothing about Greek, and many of them doubtless have felt like the principal of the University of Leyden, to whom Oliver Goldsmith applied for an appointment to teach Greek, which he had been told was a desideratum, and who said to Goldsmith: "I never learned Greek, and I do not find that I ever missed it. I have had a doctor's cap and gown without Greek; and, in short, as I do not know Greek, I do not believe that there is any good in it." That famous pronouncement upon the basis of personal ignorance buttressed by personal success is characteristic of much of the criticism of classical studies to-day. Prosperity despises uncommercial scholarship still.

We demand an education in efficiency rather than in the humanities. We measure our university curricula by the money test or the test of financial and worldly success rather than by success in making character and giving culture to the life. When Fox founded Corpus Christi College he established two chairs in Greek and in Latin in order, as he said, "to extirpate barbarism." As our colleges and universities have neglected the classics, barbarism has gradually returned; and the triumph of efficiency in the last Great War was at the same time the triumph of barbarism in Europe. The efficiency of the armies was matched only by the atrocities of the Huns on both sides of the conflict. The efficiency of organization proved to be the organization of such barbarism and savagery as the world never had seen before.

Most of the soldiers in the conflict were guiltless of any knowledge of the classical culture; and there are those who would rule all the classics out of our institutions of higher learning so that in a few generations we might be back again in the period before the Renaissance, when all Europe and America were in the Dark Ages and muddled along with little Latin and no Greek. Sir Thomas More declares that even in his day the leader of the anti-Greek party was saying, "The teachers of Greek are full-grown devils; the learners are little devils." Is that a situation devoutly to be desired? There are those who seem to think so.

They seem to think that modern science and modern efficiency will be sufficient for the modern world, and they say that we live in a scientific age, and we have plenty to do to keep up with modern discoveries without wasting any time in nosing into ancient books and dead languages. Nevertheless, we persist in thinking that it is well worth while for everyone to study this wonderful language of the

THE GREEK TESTAMENT 91

Greeks, and we suggest the following considerations as a basis for that faith.

1. It is a mistake to call the Greek a dead language. James Russell Lowell said, "Only those languages can be called dead in which nothing living was ever written," and there is truth in that statement; but there is a better reason for saying that Greek is not a dead language. It is spoken in Greece and Turkey and Asia Minor to-day. "The modern Greek has not the fineness of texture of the ancient classics, but in its essential characteristics Greek is alive to-day. Geldart, on Modern Greek, says, 'It is a strange and unparalleled fact that one of the oldest known languages of the world, a language in which the loftiest and deepest thoughts of the greatest poets, the wisest thinkers, the noblest, holiest, and best of teachers have directly or indirectly found their utterance in the far-off ages of a hoar antiquity, should be at this day the living speech of millions throughout the east of Europe, and various parts of Asia Minor and Africa; that it should have survived the fall of empires, and risen again and again from the ruin of beleaguered cities, deluged but never drowned by floods of invading barbarians, Romans, Celts, Slavs, Goths and Vandals, Avars, Huns, Franks and Turks; often

the language of the vanquished, yet never of the dead; with features seared with years and service, yet still essentially the same; instinct with the fire of life, and beautiful with the memory of the past.'"

Modern Greek resembles the classical Greek much more closely than modern Italian resembles the classical Latin, and even more closely than present-day English resembles the early classics of English literature. No other modern tongue has preserved so completely the impress of its classic beginnings. As Geldart has said, modern Greek is simply ancient Greek made easy. The modern Greek newspaper shows on every page that it is the lineal descendant of Demosthenes and Herodotus and the ancient tongue lives in its columns not only in spirit but in form.

The modern traveler in Athens buys a newspaper in the hotel and finds its news items listed under the heading, Ἀπὸ ἡμέρας εἰς ἡμέραν, "From day to day," and he may be surprised to find that there has been no change in the words and their meaning since the ancient times. He steps into the street and he finds the street names put up at the crossings and he reads Ὀδός Ἑρμοῦ, Ὀδός Ὁμήρου, Ὀδός Σωκράτου, Ὀδός Πανεπιστημίου, "Street of Hermes," "Street of Homer," "Street of Socrates," "Uni-

THE GREEK TESTAMENT

versity Street," and so on, and he finds the letters and the names to which he has always been accustomed and he feels at home at once.

He goes to the Acropolis first of all and just inside the gate he finds the sign, Ἀγαπᾶτε, φυλάττετε τὰ δένδρα, "Cherish and protect the trees." It is our sign, "Do not pick the flowers," or "Do not injure the shrubs"; but how much better it is, for those are negative and this is positive. Ἀγαπᾶτε, cherish a real affection for, literally "love" and therefore φυλάττετε, "guard," cherish, protect the flowers and shrubs and trees; exactly the same words and the same letters which were used in the classical or the New Testament times. There has been no change in them through the centuries.

Greek is no dead language. The ancient Greek seems to be a living language in Athens to-day. The traveler of the present time rides down to the Piræus and he sees on a big hoarding the English name "FORD" and before it the Greek word Αὐτοκινητάτα, and he recognizes it at once as an advertisement of a self-starting Ford; and he begins to realize that Greek is alive and not only so but quite up to date, growing and adapting itself to modern uses and conditions. It never has been a dead language and it never was more alive than to-day.

The New Testament Greek is nearer to modern Greek in its character than it is to the classical Greek, though it stands so much nearer to the classical Greek in time. That fact alone bears its witness to the most remarkable preservation of the ancient tongue in the modern speech. The ancient tongue itself never has ceased to be read and studied, unless it were in the darkest periods of the Dark Ages. It came to recognition and to new life in the Renaissance and it has lived ever since.

Bearing this fact of its present and its continuous existence in mind we go back to Lowell's contention that no language can be called dead which has immortal literature in it and we remember what Viscount Bryce said on that subject: "Let no one be afraid of the name 'dead languages.' No language is dead which perfectly conveys thoughts that are alive and are as full of energy now as they ever were. An idea or a feeling grandly expressed lives forever, and gives immortality to the words that enshrine it."[19] Alfred Noyes calls attention to the same truth: "Though Latin and Greek in a superficial sense may be 'dead languages,' they are living literature. A great work of art, statue or picture, or poem, can

---
[19] West, *The Value of the Classics*, pp. 145-146.

THE GREEK TESTAMENT

never be 'dead.' There is a confusion of thought in most of those who apply the word so glibly to the world's most vital heritage."[20] James Russell Lowell says of the Greek language and literature that it is "rammed with life, as perhaps no other writing, except Shakespeare's, ever was or will be." That was true of the ancient tongue, and that tongue is a living tongue still. Modern Greek represents it very fairly, and it is therefore of practical benefit to the traveler in the Orient to-day.

2. Greek is of practical benefit to anyone who studies it with devotion and discipline. Nothing is of more value as a preparation for any business or professional career. The president of the American Medical Association in 1914 said, "Carelessness and superficiality are incompatible with the thorough study of Latin and Greek,"[21] and if that be true, it surely would be worth while for any business or professional man to attempt at least to save himself from these things by such study.

The time was when old Doctor Snade, principal of the Royal Grammar School at London, read a note sent to him by the father of one of his students, asking the Doctor to excuse his

---
[20] West, *op. cit.*, p. 298.
[21] *Ibid.*, p. 58 and p. 249.

boy from the study of Latin, "as he did not think that Latin would be of much use to his son," and the old Doctor's eye flashed as he thundered in reply: "Not for the riches of Peru, not for the cattle on a thousand hills, not for rivers of gold, would I excuse you. If you were going to be a chimney-sweep, I would teach you mathematics, Latin, and Greek!" He surely thought that the classics were practical, and would be useful in any career.

Emerson would have sympathized with him, for he said, "Let us not forget that the adoption of the test 'What is it good for?' would abolish the rose and exalt in triumph the cabbage." The rose has its uses as well as the cabbage, and there are many who think that it represents even a higher usefulness to the race. Lowell defined a university as a place where nothing useful was taught, and he was glad of it. He was glad that there was a place where truth was sought with no ulterior motive and for itself alone, for the man who seeks truth, and truth alone, will find all other things worth while added unto him. John Fritz, the father of the steel industry in America, said, "If I had a son to be educated as an engineer, I would see to it first of all that he gained some knowledge of Latin and Greek."[22]

---
[22] West, *op. cit.*, p. 176

THE GREEK TESTAMENT 97

We heard an address by one of the leading business men in San Francisco in the course of which he said, "The lawyer you trust, the doctor you employ, the preacher you listen to, the engineer you have confidence in are men of classical training and culture. I have no hesitation in declaring that the very best preparation for a business career is a careful and thoroughgoing training in Greek." That was the opinion of a business man, and it is inevitable that a man in any professional career will soon realize his restrictions and disadvantages without the culture the study of Greek would give.

We knew a father who was too poor in his youth to get much beyond the barest fundamentals in a school education; but by close application to his books at home and by continuous practice on the battlefields of the Civil War he developed into one of the most skillful physicians and surgeons we have known. How often he has told us how he always was hampered and fettered and sometimes almost utterly discouraged by his felt need of the classics in all of his reading and study; and he was determined that at any needed sacrifice his son should have the advantages it had been impossible for him to obtain for himself. He was like the poet Whittier in that respect. Whittier called his lack of early advantages his thorn in the flesh, and he declared that it was a lifelong embarrassment and hindrance to him that he had not been privileged to study the classics in his youth.

3. The study of Greek is essential to the thorough mastery of any of the mathematical or the scientific studies of to-day. The knowledge of one science, that of grammar, all will agree can be best obtained by classical study. "The Greek directly furnishes us with three complete sciences in almost faultless form: logic, rhetoric, and geometry," and the nomenclature of all of them, whether physical or metaphysical, is borrowed from the classical tongues. To master them thoroughly we say that the study of the classics is essential. We always are ready to put that question to a practical test. Give us two students of equal capacity. Let one pursue the study of modern languages and the physical sciences exclusively; let the other in addition study the classics, and at the end of the course in nine cases out of ten the classical student will be more proficient in English and the modern tongues, and in science as well.

The testimony of the best authorities seems to be agreed at this point. The president of

THE GREEK TESTAMENT 99

the American Chemical Society in 1915–1916 said, "Taken as groups, the young men who specialized in chemistry after completing undergraduate courses including much Latin and Greek are they who have eventually risen highest."[23] The professor of geology in Princeton says, "For thirty-seven years now I have been teaching geology here, and my experience is that, taken as a group, and of course with individual exceptions, the men who do best are those who have had a broad, thorough training in Latin and Greek."[24] Classical training enabled them to excel.

Theology is a science and the mother of all the sciences, and, like all her daughters, theology derives her terminology almost wholly from the Greek. There are those who object to such long and unfamiliar terms as eschatology and soteriology and ontology and cosmology and teleology and anthropology; but to the Greek student these words are not weights but wings, accurately and adequately defining whole realms of thought. The English student is not likely to see an iota of difference between homoousios and homoiousios, but the Greek student knows at once that there is a difference there great enough to distinguish

---
[23] West, *op. cit.*, p. 65.
[24] *Ibid.*, p. 66.

orthodoxy from heterodoxy in the centuries past and in the centuries to come.

4. It is worth while for anyone to study Greek because it is essential to any mastery of our English tongue. James Russell Lowell is a good authority again. He says, "For the mastering of our own tongue there is no expedient so fruitful as translating out of another; how much more when that other is a language at once so precise and so flexible as the Greek." The truth of that proposition would seem to be self-evident. "The language cannot be separated from the ideas. In order to translate a passage from Demosthenes or Cicero, from Homer or from Horace, we must not only know the equivalent words, but we have to explore the shades of meaning to which they correspond, and the primary beliefs on which they rest. Before the beginner in classical study can choose the right meaning in the dictionary, he must have brought it home to himself, and he must know what it stands for to him personally." In this way, by careful, painstaking translation day by day, he comes to know our own language more thoroughly and more accurately than the nonclassical student ever can.

James M. Buckley tells us that through the plausible sophistries of a friend while he was

THE GREEK TESTAMENT 101

in the "veal period," as he calls it, he was led to think that he might ignore the ancient languages in getting a liberal education; but he declares that the necessity of enlarging a limited vocabulary to avoid wearisome repetitions soon taught him better. The great masters of English poetry and prose have been, almost without exception, classically trained. As Lord Brougham said in his Glasgow Inaugural, "The great things of poetry and of eloquence have been done by men who cultivated the mighty exemplars of Athenian genius, with daily and nightly devotion." Their knowledge of the Greek and Latin derivatives in our tongue and their equivalents in English gave them a richer and choicer vocabulary than others had.

The past president of the American Institute of Electrical Engineers was pleading for the study of the classics by all engineers because among other things it impressed upon the mind the great importance of precision in the expression of a thought, and he said: "Particularly in science and in engineering it is true that the best word must be found. Mere approximation is not only inadmissible, but often worse than useless. It is not sufficient that an engineer's report be so written that it can be understood; it should be so written that it cannot be misunderstood. And unquestionably it is a fact that inadequate and inaccurate statement is one of the most common and serious handicaps of the average graduate of a technological school." Was it Barrie who said that the only man in the nineteenth century who had anything to say was the scientific man; and he was the only man who did not know how to say it?[25] The study of the Greek masters would have taught him how to say it.

We talked with a Chicago lawyer who was horrified to learn that a certain theological seminary had decided no longer to require a knowledge of the Greek New Testament before graduation with their degree and he said: "The training in accuracy of expression which a study of the Greek language and literature alone can give is absolutely necessary in preparation for a successful legal career, and I should think that it would be still more important in the pulpit. Sometimes in the making of wills or other legal documents the disposition of a million dollars may depend upon the right use of a single word and the classically trained lawyer will know how to use it when his more ignorant colleague will be likely to fail. In the law such great and important

---
[25]West, *op. cit.*, pp. 71, 72.

THE GREEK TESTAMENT 103

interests are often concerned in the right and wrong use of words, and I should think that that would be even more true in the work of the ministry." He was right. Millions of money may be lost in the careless use of words in the law; many a soul has been lost through the careless use of words in the pulpit.

Henry Cabot Lodge, in defending the usefulness of the classics, said, "Take the learned professions. Surely it is well that the clergy should have some knowledge of the language of the New Testament and of that other in which a large part of the Christian world repeat their prayers and read their Bibles. It cannot be wholly without value to physicians and surgeons to be acquainted with the language and the literature of the race among whom their noble and beneficent profession finds its birthplace or of the language in which they still write their prescriptions, or of both these languages in which they bring forth for their new drugs and new diseases names which not infrequently they mispronounce." They cannot avoid their use.

In connection with this statement by Senator Lodge it may be interesting to note that "in Dunglison's medical dictionary there are approximately forty-one thousand words, of which twenty thousand are derived from the

Greek and twenty-one thousand from the Latin, French, Saxon, and English."[26]

Senator Lodge went on to say: "Lawyers no doubt can make a living, and often a very good one, knowing only the statutes and the more obvious rules of pleading and practice. But it can hardly be questioned that if they go beyond this limited region, a familiarity with the language which enshrines the maxims they quote, and in which is written that great system of jurisprudence bequeathed to us by the Romans and still followed in most countries of western civilization, is not only useful but desirable.

"If we turn to the higher sciences, we find a like condition. The astronomer cannot explore the heavens without seeing the beautiful mythology of Greece forever written in the stars. The Greek alphabet figures in his catalogues and calculations, and some of his greatest forerunners wrote in Latin. The naturalists, the botanists, the geologists, the biologists, not only owe their very names to the classics which some of them despise, but it would not come amiss if they knew, as no doubt many of them do, something of the languages from which they take their nomenclatures and of the literatures where appear the

---
[26] West, *op. cit.*, p. 255.

THE GREEK TESTAMENT 105

first guesses at scientific truths and the first and often very brilliant speculations as to the secrets of the universe. In philology, anthropology, and archæology a knowledge of Latin and Greek is, of course, essential. As to literature, it is needless to argue. A literary man should know something of literature, and literature includes the writings of Greece and Rome. In all these instances which I have cited it is difficult to find justification for asserting that the study of the classics is a waste of time because they are useless in after life."[27]

The classics are useful in preparation for a business or a professional career, and they are useful not least in the aid which they give to accurate English expression. Here, then, is a reason which appeals to everyone who cares to use his own tongue effectively either in public speech or in written composition. That ought to include everyone, without exception.

5. Possibly the best and abiding reason for the study of the Greek language by us to-day is that it is essential to a liberal education. Culture, genuine literary culture, is impossible without some knowledge of the scientific, philosophical, and literary achievements of the Greeks. President Buttz, of Drew Theological Seminary, said, "I am well convinced that so

[27] West, *op. cit.*, pp. 109-110.

long as highest poetry shall be read, so long as oratory shall be cherished, so long as the beautiful in art and literature shall be admired among men, so long must scholars appreciate and study the Greek."

President Gilman, of Johns Hopkins University, in defining the acquirements of a man of liberal education, said, "His knowledge should consist of the workings of body and mind, and should include not only an understanding of his mother tongue, its history and capabilities, but of at least two other tongues; and with scientific learning should be combined a knowledge of the literature of the world, together with universal history and political economy." He holds therefore that, with a due regard to physical culture, the groundwork of a modern liberal education should be mathematics, languages (ancient and modern), history, political science, and philosophy. As we run through that list we see at once that Greek is essential to the mastery of every one of these subjects, while as a language and in its literature it furnishes a large and an essential measure of culture itself.

Nicholas Murray Butler, president of Columbia University, thinks that a knowledge of the classics is necessary for any "sure standard for the determination and the ap-

THE GREEK TESTAMENT 107

preciation of excellence in letters and in art,"[28] and surely these things are the essential results of any true culture. Alexander Duane declares: "The study of the Greek language and literature, in the original, bringing us into intimate contact with the Greek mind, fulfills better than anything that has yet been devised the prime objects of education—information, mental culture, mental discipline and the promotion of high ideals. There is, indeed, no greater training for the mind than is furnished by the study of the Greek language and the translation of Greek originals; and, the Bible and Shakespeare apart, there is no more potent means of mental culture and spiritual uplift than is furnished by Greek literature."[29]

"Special culture," says Lowell, "is the gymnastic of the mind, but liberal culture is its healthy exercise in the open air. Train your mental muscles faithfully for the particular service to which you intend to develop them in the great workshop of active life, but do not forget to take your constitutional among the classics, no matter in what language. That is the kind of atmosphere to oxygenate the blood, and keep the brain wholesome." The Greeks lived in the open air and the sunshine.

---
[28] West, *op. cit.*, p. 44.
[29] *Ibid.*, pp. 257–258.

They were the people of the Olympian and Isthmian games. They devoted themselves to the culture of body and mind. Their tongue was a healthy and wholesome tongue.

"It is the nearest perfection of all of the languages, and offers the finest field for exercise in the most delicate forms of expression." He who masters it comes into the possession, as Gibbon said, "of a golden key that can unlock the treasures of antiquity, of a musical and prolific language that gives a soul to the objects of sense and a body to the abstractions of philosophy."[30] Even a little knowledge is worth while. "A little is a big per cent on nothing," as John A. Broadus used to say.[31] When Doctor Furness was making a farewell address to the students of the University of Pennsylvania he said to them, "If you cannot drink deep out of the Pierian spring, in heaven's name, take a sip."[32]

The literature built up in this language has been a mental and spiritual tonic to all time. The language is worth while in itself as a mental and spiritual discipline, but we study it and cherish it to-day because of its literature.

---

[30] Gibbon, *Rome*, chap. lxvi, vol. iv, p. 445.

[31] Robertson, *The Minister and His Greek New Testament*, p. 15. George H. Doran Company. Used by permission.

[32] West, *op. cit.*, p. 343.

THE GREEK TESTAMENT

A wonderful land, a wonderful people, an unrivaled tongue; we have glanced at these simply by way of introduction to the wonderful literature which above all else has made all these a living force and a felt power in the world to our day.

PART IV

A WONDERFUL LITERATURE

It is one of the marvels of world history how, in the providence of God, to some single nation or people has been intrusted the perfect development of some one of the great principles necessary to world advancement, some one side of human aspiration and inspiration, an essential element of social and soul progress and success. On the banks of the Tiber rose the imperial city of Rome. Within her walls a code of civil government was perfected which made a state of supreme centralized power whose executive control through flawless channels made itself felt and feared, respected and trusted through every rank of society from the haughtiest noble on the Esquiline hill to the poorest serf in the remotest confines of conquered territory. The Roman legions and the Roman Cæsars carried this principle of law and order, their examples of civil codes and good government, beyond Roman walls through all the world.

On the plains of Palestine dwelt a people,

THE GREEK TESTAMENT 111

for long, long centuries the most isolated and exclusive of all known peoples—the hermit nation of ancient times, self-centered and self-satisfied, a whole people of saints and seers, psalmists and prophets, whose kings were the anointed of the Lord, whose poorest peasants were chosen vessels called to stand on his holy hill, to whom all other peoples were Gentile dogs, unfit for association, amalgamation, reformation, wedded to their idolatries, under the wrath of the one true God. Among these exclusive Jews the religious idea was fostered, monotheism and theocracy became essentials of the national life, and in the fullness of time "there arose, in all the force of living conviction, a faith the most unrestricted, the most expansive, and all-embracing which the world had known or ever can know"; and from among these exclusive Jews went forth Peter and Paul and the missionary apostles carrying the Christian doctrine and the catholic faith beyond the borders of Palestine into all the world.

What Rome did for civil government, what Palestine did for the religious principle, that did the Greeks do for the æsthetic faculty and the intellectual culture of the world. Greece came at last to that high pitch of mental vigor which fitted her to be the divinely appointed teacher of the surrounding nations and even of the ends of the earth. The Cæsars spread Roman polity through Europe into Asia and Africa. Paul the apostle carried Christianity from Asia to Europe, and thence its influence became world-wide. That the knowledge of the products of Greek intellect and culture might likewise spread over the globe a man must be found who would combine in himself the characteristics of both the imperial Cæsar and the apostle Paul, some man with a military genius sufficient to command the respect of all men for the language, the nation, the literature he might represent and at the same time with a fervid love of and an apostolic devotion to that language and its best literature, which would in itself be a sufficient guarantee to all men of their transcendent excellence. Such a man was Alexander the Great.

World conqueror, his military genius speaks for itself. The pupil of Aristotle, he carried a copy of Homer with him through all his campaigns, sent back to his teacher from each conquered province rare collections of animals and plants, spared the house of the poet Pindar when all the rest of Thebes was destroyed, spread the Greek language and literature wherever his victorious armies came, was the

THE GREEK TESTAMENT 113

patron of every art and science, the civilizer and benefactor of every land he entered upon, displaying everywhere his love for literature, and showing that "sense of the noble and great which distinguishes Alexander from all the conquerors who have only swept like a hurricane through the world." Of his many mighty deeds we shall note but one.

At the western mouth of the Nile he found the village of Rakotis, "an Egyptian post to prevent the ingress of strangers." Directed to it, as Plutarch tells us, by a dream in which an old man of venerable aspect stood by his bedside and recited from Homer,

"High o'er a gulfy sea the Parthian Isle
Fronts the deep roar of disemboguing Nile,"

he at once recognized its admirable situation for all the purposes he had in mind.[1] As though by magic on the village site rose a great city, "itself a monument of engineering and architectural skill"; destined to be the commercial entrepôt between the eastern and the western world; intended by its founder to be a new center of intellectual life to the globe.

In all respects the city named after himself came near the fulfillment of his heart's desire. Alexandria was soon in the extent of its com-

[1] Plutarch, *Alexander*, p. 443.

merce the rival, successor, and superior of Tyre; was soon in its supremacy in the world of mind the rival, successor, and almost the equal of Athens itself in its zenith of power. In the days when the Greek language was spoken from the Danube to India there was no more characteristically Greek city than the Egyptian city of Alexandria. In the third century B. C. it was the most important center of Greek culture, and for two hundred years it maintained itself as the intellectual center of the world.

Of the many and costly works in this commanding city we note but one: the Museum, so called. The Ptolemaic successors of the great conqueror followed the example he had set in the patronage of literature, science, and art. Under their fostering care the Alexandrian Museum became the great University of the East, in whose astronomical observatories, chemical laboratories, and lecture rooms were gathered the accumulated treasures of knowledge from all the earth. Its fame brought students and professors from all parts of the world, as many as fourteen thousand being present at one time.

The world has had great universities, at Athens, at Bagdad and Cordova, at Paris and Oxford and Berlin; but the world never has

THE GREEK TESTAMENT 115

seen a university so thoroughly equipped with all available advantages and so widely influential as was in its day the great Museum of Alexandria. Says Thalheimer's history, "No spot ever witnessed more literary and intellectual activity. There Euclid first unfolded the Elements of Geometry; Eratosthenes discoursed of Geography; Hipparchus of Astronomy; Aristophanes and Aristarchus of Criticism; Manetho of History; while Apelles and Antiphilus added their paintings, and Philetas and Callimachus and Apollonius their poems, for the delight of a court whose monarch was himself an author, and in which talent constituted rank." To the names here given many more might be added: such as Lycophron, Theocritus, Nicander, Homer the son of Macro, Theodosius, Theon, and Hypatia. These may well suffice.

August Boeckh was the man who made a passionate classicist out of an amateurish student of literature in the person of Professor Gildersleeve, who speaks of "the orbed completeness of the ideal he evoked,"[2] and it is said that Boeckh's general characterization of antiquity never has been surpassed. In speaking of the Alexandrian Museum he said,

---
[2]Gildersleeve, *Hellas and Hesperia*, p. 42. Henry Holt & Co. Used by permission.

"Science had previously been carried on by individual investigators working in isolation; and in the schools of philosophy and rhetoric a single teacher was the nucleus of a group of pupils who studied with him alone; but in the Museum of Alexandria we have the first establishment of a great scientific community, which in turn became the model of similar foundations elsewhere."[3]

Of the many departments of this great university we note but one: the great Library, "the pride and boast of antiquity." Demetrius Phalareus was commissioned to collect all the writings in the world. The librarians were appointed and salaried by the emperors. Government agents ransacked all Europe and Asia for every literary work of value, with instructions to secure all such at any cost. An embargo was laid upon all books, whether public or private property, which entered Alexanandria. The originals were retained, unscrupulously enough. Copies were made, and a copy was in mock generosity returned to the owner.

In this way autograph copies of Æschylus, Sophocles, and Euripides were obtained from the Athenians. A deposit of one hundred talents of silver was made at the time of their

---

[3]Cooper, *op. cit.*, p. 112.

THE GREEK TESTAMENT 117

loan, and this sum was forfeited by the king. The originals were retained at Alexandria and copies were sent back to Athens. Thus by fair means and foul a great collection of seven hundred thousand volumes was made. It was, as Dieterich says, "the great culture-reservoir of the Greek-Oriental world." Nothing like it ever had been seen in the ancient days; nothing like it in the completeness of its collection, in the all-comprehensiveness of its representation of world literature, ever will be seen again.

It had but one rival, in the library of Eumenes the Second at Pergamus in Mysia; but in the course of events the two hundred thousand volumes collected there were removed to Alexandria; and from that time the city of the Macedonian king became the chief and only seat of letters and art, the chief and only center of refinement, the world's resort for literary and scientific men. Professor Mahaffy while lecturing in Chicago in 1904 said, "There can be no doubt that the creation of the great cosmopolitan library at Alexandria, and the great trade in books which came thence, were the greatest acts of protection ever done for the greatest literature the world has seen." Why have we dwelt at such length upon this city, this university, this library?

Because here, and here alone, through all the ages and in all the world, could we say, "Behold Greek literature complete: behold Greek literature in the concrete!"

We shall now enter this library to take one glance at least upon Greek literature as it once was, as it never will be again. From either the royal palace or the Museum proper long colonnades of the most costly marble, adorned with obelisks and sphinxes, the spoil of the cities of the Pharaohs, lead into the library room. There are rolls upon rolls, papyrus and parchment, Diphterai and Charta, books of skins and books of scrolls, thousands upon thousands, seven hundred thousand in all; carefully guarded by custodians, under the superintending eye of the royal librarian, open to the philosophers, lecturers, students of every class, read, studied, commented upon. The scholia of the Alexandrian grammarians are an invaluable treasure to the Greek students of to-day. The chief librarian not only collected and catalogued all the books of the Greek literature but he instituted researches into the purity of the text. Our texts of the classics represent the pruning process undergone here at Alexandria. Our Homer probably is one sixth less in size than the pre-Alexandrine text with its many un-

THE GREEK TESTAMENT 119

authorized additions. Here or in this vicinity was the Septuagint translation of the Jewish Scriptures made, an accomplishment which lays the Christian world under obligation to these indefatigable workers.

Seven hundred thousand volumes, here first collected and critically studied in close comparison with each other! Greek literature was complete. Here on these library walls were the representatives of perfected literary form, marked in composition and material with a chaste simplicity and majestic energy no other age could equal. The best that could be done with that tongue and among that people had been done. Only one book hereafter would be added in this Greek speech which would in any sense rival, equal, and surpass those which had gone before in stirring the world's thought and in reaching and influencing the world's heart and mind. With that single exception all worthy Greek literature was collected within these library walls. Nothing remained but to catalogue and cherish it here.

The work of cataloguing was accomplished by Aristophanes in the reign of Ptolemy Euergetes and by Aristarchus his disciple and successor. They did more than that. They made what is known as the Alexandrian Canon, forever to distinguish the great classical authors from the herd of inferior writers in the same tongue. Just as the canons of the Old Testament and of the New Testament rule out forever from the sacred books all apocryphal writings and those of evidently inferior literary style which have at any time laid claim to divine inspiration and a consequent right to a place among the sacred rolls, so this Alexandrian Canon was intended to bar out forever as authorities for allowed idiom and verbal purity as well as models of literary style the hosts of inferior works which disputed with the masters for a permanent hold on the race and which, the grammarians thought, were corrupting and would continue to corrupt the purity of the tongue made sacred by the use and example of Homer, Æschylus, and Plato.

The authority of the Canon has been recognized in the literary world from that day to this. The authors it included in its list have been regarded ever since as the leaders of thought and masters of form among the Greeks. Possibly some authors were omitted who should have been admitted. Perhaps there are those whose books would have been equally valued and valuable, but whose works have been allowed to perish because they were liable to greater neglect through their ex-

THE GREEK TESTAMENT 121

clusion from the Canon; but while that may be true, we may at the same time be sure that the authors included in the Canon of Alexandria were thereby stamped with an authority, a dignity, an almost divinity which secured for them everywhere respect and reverent handling, and an attempt at careful preservation through the centuries down to even our day.

Not all of these survive, as is at once apparent as we read through the list. The Canon made ten divisions of authors. 1. The Epic Poets: Homer, Hesiod, Pisander, Panyasis, and Antimachus. 2. The Iambic Poets: Archilochus, Simonides, and Hipponax. 3. The Lyric Poets: Alcman, Alcæus, Sappho, Stesichorus, Pindar, Bacchylides, Ibycus, Anacreon, Simonides. 4. The Elegiac Poets: Callinus, Mimnermus, Philetas, Callimachus. 5. The Tragic Poets: Æschylus, Sophocles, Euripides, Ion, Achæus, Agathon. To these they added a second class: Alexander, Philiscus, Sositheus, Homer the younger, Æantides, Sosiphanes, Lycophron. 6. The Comic Poets: Epicharmus, Eupolis, Aristophanes, Pherecrates, Plato, Antiphanes, Alexis, Menander, Philippides, Diphilus, Philemon, Apollodorus. 7. The Historians: Herodotus, Thucydides, Xenophon, Theopompus, Ephorus, Philistus, Anaximenes,

Callisthenes. 8. The Orators: Antiphon, Andocides, Lysias, Isocrates, Isæus, Æschines, Lycurgus, Demosthenes, Hyperides. Dinarchus. 9. The Philosophers: Plato, Xenophon, Æschines Socraticus, Aristotle, Theophrastus. 10. Seven contemporaries, called from their number the Poetic Pleiades: Apollonius, Aratus, Philiscus, Homer the younger, Lycophron, Nicander, Theocritus.

That Alexandrian Canon is unique in the literary world. Where else can we find a whole literature brought together under careful and competent examination and an authoritative list of its seventy-five best writers published to the world and the list accepted by the world as authoritative for centuries on centuries? In this day, when every first-, second-, third-, and fifth-rate writer makes his own list of The Hundred Best Books and we find on comparison of the numerous and numberless lists of The Hundred Best Books that they already are several thousand in number, it is refreshing to find one complete national literature with its seventy-five most worthy representatives universally acknowledged.

Another noteworthy fact connected with this Alexandrian Canon is this: of the seventy-five authors it includes, the works either in whole or in part of only twenty-five are now

THE GREEK TESTAMENT 123

extant. The Alexandrian Library was burned and wholly destroyed in civil broils and national wars, by Christian and Moslem fanatics and the brutal soldier's torch. Most of the seven hundred thousand volumes have disappeared from the earth. Of many not even the title remains, and no slightest record on any page of history. Many of them of course were no serious loss; but these seventy-five authors—what an invaluable treasure they would be!

Niebuhr, the German historian, writes, "It is said that a philologer once tried to conjure up spirits in order to obtain from them ancient books which were lost; and if such a thing were possible, the first ancient work to be asked for would be the Origenes of Cato; for if we had them, and the history of Quintus Fabius Pictor, we might dispense with all speculations concerning the early history of the nations of Italy." If such a thing were possible, if we were a conjurer able to call back into existence ancient books which were lost, we would pass by Cato's Origenes and all Latin literature, not being particularly interested in the early history of the nations of Italy. We would go back to that nobler race and better time, to that language and literature which "as an instrument of human feeling was as capable of sweet and tender expression as any mellow old Stradivarius responsive to the genius of a Paganini, and as an instrument of human thought once had for philosophical discrimination and combat as wondrous edge and temper as any old Damascus blade." We would ask for the lost works of Æschylus and Aristotle.

Have we ever thought of it seriously, have we ever realized it as we should, that, enthusiastic as we are and we ought to be over these ancient literatures, we have them and admire them only in a mutilated and fragmentary form? In the canonical books of the Old Testament we read about the Book of Josiah and the Book of Jehu, the Book of the Constitution of the Kingdom, and the Book of the Wars of the Lord, the Acts of Solomon, the Prophecy of Nathan, the Visions of Iddo, the Sayings of the Seers; but these books are nowhere found. The existing Hebrew literature is but a portion of that which the Hebrews once had.

Look at the Latin histories, to mention but one division of that literature. Rich portions of Livy, Tacitus, Polybius, Dion Cassius, Dionysius of Halicarnassus have perished. Latin literature is forever and irretrievably bereft. Even so in the Greek, in many of our texts whole passages are gone; in the history

THE GREEK TESTAMENT   125

of its literature we find that whole books are missing; and many of its authors live now only in name. Some nine hundred tragedies were produced in Athens and we have only thirty-three of them.

Gilbert Murray, Regius Professor of Greek in Oxford University, says: "Æschylus wrote ninety plays; the Alexandrians possessed seventy-two of them; we have seven. Sophocles wrote one hundred and twenty-three; . . . we have seven. Euripides wrote ninety-two; Alexandria possessed seventy-eight; we have nineteen. Of Pindar, the Alexandrians possessed seventeen books; we have four, not complete. . . . Of Alcman they had six, of Alcæus at least ten, of Sappho nine; we have none. They had twenty-six books of Stesichorus; we have none. They had the books of Heraclitus, Empedocles, Parmenides, Anaxagoras. They had the splendid mass of Chrysippus. They had Dicæarchus' Life of Hellas; they had the great scientific and imaginative works of Eratosthenes; they had the thirty books of Ephorus' universal history, the twelve books of Theopompus' Hellenica and the fifty-six of his Philippica. Of all which tradition has brought us nothing."

Chœrilus competed with Æschylus and took the prize away from him thirteen times, and he wrote one hundred and fifty dramas in all, and not one of the one hundred and fifty is now in existence. No one can tell how great our loss has been in the failure to preserve them. It is altogether possible that some of the dramas which we know only by name were superior to some of those we have. The Œdipus Tyrannus of Sophocles was defeated by a play of Philocles, of which we have no fragment remaining. Euphorion and Xenocles and Nichomachus were each victorious over Euripides; but the plays which won the verdict in their favor are all lost. Gratinus defeated Aristophanes and gained the prize nine times, but none of his plays are now extant.

If we could give reality to that picture of the Alexandrian Museum, with its seven hundred thousand volumes in tangible existence on the walls, we might have some conception of what Greek literature in its verity was. If the seventy-five authors of the Alexandrian Canon were fully represented on our own library shelves, we might know Greek literature in its completed magnificence, in all the rounded, perfected grandeur of the whole; but our fragments of the literature are like our fragments of the art.

Over in Rome is the torso of the Belvedere, attributed to Apollonius of Athens. It is

THE GREEK TESTAMENT 127

only a mutilated trunk; but every line left in it is instinctive with the superlative inspiration known only to those old Greeks. The art critics say that it presents a "harmonious union of majesty, grandeur, and breadth of composition, united to exactness of detail so truthful in the minutest particulars and so full of ease, grace, and vitality" that the imagination, inspired by its exquisite though colossal proportions, easily invests it with its original perfection. Heine stands before the Venus of the Louvre and weeps; for the mutilated goddess is still divine. We only imagine its original strength.

So we turn to the twenty-five authors of the Canon whose works in part or in whole still survive; and in them we catch the inspiration which breathed in all, from them we can imagine what the original perfection must have been. We cannot take time to review these twenty-five authors and their works. We wish we could. We will say now only this, that no library is complete without these greatest of the classics on its shelves, and no education is complete without an intimate acquaintance with these books either in the original or in translation. We glance at a few of the great names.

We begin with Homer. In Hogg's *Life of*

Shelley we read of that English clergyman who "devoted all his waking hours for thirty years to a regular course of Greek writers. He arranged them in a three years' series, and when they were ended he began again. The only exception was in the case of Homer, whose works he read every year for a month at the seashore—'the proper place to read Homer,' he said; and, as he also pointed out, there were twenty-four week-days in a month, and by taking a book of the *Iliad* before dinner, and a book of the *Odyssey* after dinner, he just finished his pleasant task. On rainy days, when he could not walk, he threw in the Homeric Hymns; he, moreover, read a newspaper once a week, and occasionally ran through a few pages of Virgil and Cicero, just to satisfy himself that it was a waste of time for anyone who could read Greek to look at anything else. Simple and perennial felicity: no vacillation, no variableness or shadow of turning; no doubting between literature and science, still less between this or that department of literature."

It is a magnificent literature, the ancient literature of the Greeks, even in its present fragmentary and imperfect form; and it is one of the marvels and mysteries of world history that, unlike the early writings of other

THE GREEK TESTAMENT 129

peoples, the literature of the Greeks begins with one perfect work of art. No Greek writer ever surpassed Homer. Homer must be read by everyone who makes any pretense to scholarship, for he is the greatest of the poets, the greatest writer in the literature of the ancient and the modern world. Daniel Steele once said: "Homer is both the fountain and the standard of poetry. The afflatus of all the modern poets is breathed by him. The visitor to London will find on the base of that poem in marble, the Albert Memorial in Hyde Park, an artist's conception wondrously beautiful and truthful. It is a group of the world's greatest poets, in life size, among them Virgil, Dante, Chaucer, Shakespeare, Milton, Molière, and Cervantes, all listening entranced to an old bard in the midst who is touching the strings of his lyre. Well may England give the place of honor to Homer, the tutor who has trained in her universities that succession of illustrious statesmen and orators of whom Gladstone was a representative. That grand old man said he wanted to do two things before he died—give home rule to Ireland, and prove the identity of Homeric and Hebrew theology. The writers of the golden age of English literature, and especially the giants of the English pulpit and Parliament, were nurtured almost entirely upon the Bible and the classics of the Greek."

Matthew Arnold declared that there never was any such naturally gifted poet as Shakespeare, but he went on to say, "Homer leaves Shakespeare, with all his unequaled gifts, as far behind as perfection leaves imperfection." Look over the list of the English poets—Milton, Gray, Shelley, Keats, Landor, Tennyson, Browning, Matthew Arnold, Swinburne, Bridges—and anyone who is acquainted with their works and familiar with the Greek classics realizes at once the great indebtedness of all of them to the Greek masters.

In the Louvre there is a great painting by Ingres, with the title, Homer Deified. At present it is detached from the wall and given the most prominent position at the end of the long hall. Homer sits on the central throne and all the poets—Æschylus, Sophocles, Shakespeare, Dante, Racine, Molière and the others—are grouped about him and subordinated to him; and the Greek motto is written beneath, "If Homer is a god, let us worship him. If Homer is not a god, νομιζέσθω, let us reckon him to be a god." It is a French exaggeration of the same reverence for the greatest master of literature which is expressed in the Albert Memorial in London. Paul Elmer

THE GREEK TESTAMENT 131

More declares, "The *Iliad* and the *Odyssey* have a beauty and humanity that no modern epic poet has ever touched—not Milton himself, though I adore Milton this side of idolatry."[4] Phidias got his conception of Zeus from Homer; and the *Iliad* and the *Odyssey* were the Bible of the Greeks for centuries.

Richard Salter Storrs, of New York, was called "the prince of pulpit rhetoricians"; and it was said of him that "as an orator for occasions of an elevated character, he was perhaps as near as any living American the elect favorite voice of the nation." Standing then at the pinnacle of ministerial fame and wide-extended usefulness, it is interesting for us to notice that the two elements of his power were said to be his moral earnestness and an elegance of culture formed upon the epideictic models of the ancient Greeks. He was a lover of Homer and of all Greek literature. We quote a paragraph from his Phi Beta Kappa oration at Harvard, descriptive of the impressions made by the *Iliad*, and illustrative of the Greek influence upon his spirit and style.

He says: "The wine-colored waters, breaking around the high-beaked ships; the camp fires glittering on the plain; the splendor of armor shining in the air, as with the flash of moun-

[4]West, *op. cit.*, p. 290.

tain fires; the troubled dust rising in mist before the tramp of rapid feet; greaves with their silver clasps; helmets crested with their horsehair plumes; the marvelous shield with triple-border blazoned with manifold intricate device, and circled by the ocean stream; the changeful flight, the anguish and rage, and the illustrious funeral pile"—these are beautiful, wondrously so, but "not by these though moving before us in epic verse, and touched by iridescent lights by the magic of genius, is the mind held captive to the *Iliad*," not by these, but "by its shadowy morning-time 'spirit of surmise and aspiration,' by the tender and daring divine illusions, which see the air quick with veiled Powers, and the responding earth the haunted field of their Olympian struggle and debate." The whole paragraph is Homeric, filled with Homer's adjectives and Homer's similes.

"To be Homeric," says Coleridge, "is to be natural, lively, rapid, energetic, harmonious." Daniel Steele advises, "Would a preacher cultivate his imagination, guarding against extravagance? Let him read Homer." Alcibiades went to a school and asked for Homer's *Iliad* and the schoolmaster said, "We do not keep Homer here." Alcibiades then knocked the schoolmaster down and went on. He was a man of hot passions and that was his method of protest against any school which would leave Homer out of its curriculum.[5] What authors did they study in that school? All of them were inferior to Homer. Æschylus spoke for them all when he said that in his own work he simply served up "fragments from the feast of Homer." We ought to begin with Homer. We ought to be acquainted with his style and his figures of speech. We ought to be able to understand references to him and to recognize quotations from him. We ought to be able to make constant use of him in our own literary labor.

Beginning with him, we will read on into Æschylus and Sophocles and Euripides: Æschylus, full of gorgeous imagery and magnificent expressions, fond of metaphorical phrases and strange compounds, displaying the strong feelings and impulses, describing the awful and the terrible, with gods for characters and superhuman action and suffering; Sophocles, whose tragedies are not only the perfection of the Greek drama but also approach as nearly as is conceivable to the perfect ideal of that species of poetry, with more sympathy and personality than Æschylus, and so bringing his characters and the lesson they

[5]Plutarch, *Alc.* 3.

teach close home to the human heart; Euripides, holding the mirror up to nature, reflecting her very form and figure, full of tenderness and pathos, the chosen model of Cicero and Quintillian.

Browning said of Æschylus,

"Æschylus' bronze-throat eagle-bark at blood
Has somehow spoilt my taste for twitterings."

Livingstone declares, "It is impossible to appreciate Æschylus in a translation, nor can the impression he creates be put into words. Some idea may be got from the epithets which critics use of him—sublime, grand, dithyrambic, colossal, elemental, titanic, superhuman. Milton at his grandest, Marlowe at moments, Shakespeare when he shows us the mad Lear in the storm on the moor or Macbeth with the witches on the 'blasted heath,' Victor Hugo in certain passages of La Légende des Siècles, come nearest to him."[6]

Sophocles, dear to the gods and loved of all men, the favorite of fortune in all his long life, beautiful in face and form and equally beautiful in soul and mind, twenty times the winner of the first prize in the great annual competition in Athens, unspoiled and well-poised, living happily and dying peacefully, funda-

---
[6]Livingstone, *The Pageant of Greece*, p. 113.

mentally religious and embodying the imperishable features of his nation's faith in the perfect products of his poetic genius, will live in history as one of the ideal figures of Hellenic literature and life.

Euripides, on the other hand, was the skeptic and the philosopher, encyclopedic in his interests and reproducing on his stage almost every idea of importance in the previous theology and ethics of the people, while he introduced them to almost every phase of the present-day philosophy and speculation, younger than Sophocles and older than Socrates, while contemporary with them both, the only dramatist whose plays ever attracted Socrates to the theater, and the most beloved and generally popular of the great tragedians, as is shown in the multitude of quotations from him in the works of other writers and in the fact that more than twice as many of his tragedies have survived to our time as of Æschylus and Sophocles combined. These dramatists were the great exponents of patriotism and religion and ethics and art. They philosophized upon the most profound problems of human existence and national destiny. They were among the most influential forces in the national life.

Leaving the Tragic Three we will read on

into Plato and Xenophon. "The very spirit and essence of philosophy move in beautiful forms before our eyes" through all the *Dialogues* and the *Memorabilia,* W. S. Tyler, professor of Greek at Amherst, has written. "No tragedy of Sophocles has a more dramatic structure, no comedy of Aristophanes a more pleasing dialogue, no epic of Homer or lyric of Anacreon more grace and affluence of language, no temple or statue in all Greece a more artistic form and finish than the Dialogues of Plato."

We remember what Emerson said about Plato: "Plato stands between the truth and every man's mind and has almost impressed language and the primary forms of thought with his name and seal. . . . Out of Plato come all things that are still written and debated among men of thought. . . . Plato is at once the glory and the shame of mankind, since neither Saxon nor Roman has availed to add any idea to his categories. . . . These sentences contain the culture of the nations; these are the corner-stone of the schools; these are the fountainhead of literature. A discipline it is in logic, arithmetic, taste, symmetry, poetry, language, rhetoric, ontology, morals or practical wisdom. There was never such range of speculation. . . . His

THE GREEK TESTAMENT 137

book has been the Bible of the learned for twenty-two hundred years. Boethius, Rabelais, Erasmus, Bruno, Locke, Rousseau, Alfieri, Coleridge are readers of Plato and translate his good things into the vernacular. Saint Augustine, Copernicus, Newton, Behmen, Swedenborg, Goethe are his debtors and must say after him. . . . The Alexandrians were Platonists, the Elizabethans no less. Plato's Phædo contains Calvinism; Christianity is in it. Mahometanism draws all its philosophy from him. Mysticism finds in Plato all its texts."[7]

A writer in Lippincott's dictionary has said: "No philosopher, of whatever age or nation, has contributed so much as Plato toward the moral and intellectual culture of the human race. This preeminence is due not solely to his transcendent intellect or to the marvelous depth and comprehensiveness of his philosophic views, but also in no small measure to his poetic power and to that unrivaled grace and beauty of style which led the ancients to say that if Jove should speak Greek he would speak like Plato."[8] It is small wonder that Clement of Alexandria was ready to declare that Plato wrote "by inspiration of God," or

---
[7] Emerson, *Representative Men*, pp. 41, 42.
[8] Martin, *op. cit.*, p. 45.

that Augustine believed that "only a few words and phrases" needed to be changed to bring Platonism into complete accord with Christianity.

Then we will read the Anabasis, "one of the most fascinating books in the world," says Professor Jebb, the story of the march of the ten thousand Greeks, a mere handful among the millions of Persia, into the very center of the dominions of the Great King, the king of many realms, mocking him and his power in his very presence, at his very gates, and then marching back again, surrounded by superior numbers, through hostile lands, by new and untried ways, in the midst of opposing nations, forcing a triumphant passage everywhere, over rivers and mountains, back to safety and the sea.

After the Anabasis, Xenophon's *Memorabilia;* the pen-picture of that greatest figure among the Greeks, mighty in argument, master among men, prince of moralists, the pioneer of philosophy and yet the peer of any and all the philosophers who have followed him, a devotee and an apostle of the truth, the most influential thinker the world has produced. He had great physical strength and great personal fascinations. He was a creative genius, uniting intellectual depth and moral enthusiasm, a prophet and a martyr, ugly, witty, sublime: a man of whom Xenophon says, "No one ever heard him say or saw him do anything impious or profane";[9] of whom Plato writes, "He was the best man, I think, that I have ever known, the wisest too and the most just";[10] of whom Professor Seymour declares, "No other man ever influenced so profoundly the course of the world's thoughts"; and of whom Rabbi Screiber has dared to affirm, "There is a man who for purity of motive, for courage of his opinions, and loftiness of thought, and all the attributes which go to make a true man, has been surpassed by no man in history; and had he lived among the Jews, they would have made him their Messiah. This man died for his faith; and yet he remained simple Socrates." The *Memorabilia* is a monument to his memory, the record of this man's daily conversations and life.

Xenophon closed that record with these words: "To me, personally, he was what I have endeavored to describe; so pious and devoutly religious that he would take no step apart from the will of heaven; so just and upright that he never did even a trifling injury to any

---
[9] Xenophon, *Memorabilia*, i, 20.
[10] Plato, *Phædo*, 118B.

living soul; so self-controlled, so temperate, that he never at any time chose the sweeter in place of the better; so sensible and wise and prudent that in distinguishing the better from the worse he never erred. . . . With these characteristics, he seemed to me to be the very impersonation of human perfection and happiness."[11]

He was the master of Plato and the gadfly of Athens. He believed that it was better to obey God than man, and he was a martyr to that faith. Grote, the historian of Greece, pays this tribute to Socrates as a teacher of morals, "Where are we to look for a parallel to Socrates? No man has ever been found strong enough to bend his bow. . . . He is the only cross-examining missionary in history. . . . Socrates enlarged the horizon, improved the method, and multiplied the ascendant minds of Greece in a manner never since paralleled by any moral teacher."[12]

In the camp at Potidæa he stood in a trance for twenty-four hours and he came out of that psychological experience to devote himself without ceasing to the conversion of his fellow citizens to the highest wisdom in conduct and life. There never was a more successful

---
[11] Xenophon, *Memorabilia*, iv, 8. 11.
[12] Martin, *op. cit.*, p. 184.

preacher and teacher. He elevated the thought of his contemporaries and influenced for good all succeeding generations.

In his defense before his judges he stated his mission and position as follows: "If you say to me, Socrates, this time you shall be let off, but upon one condition, that you are not to inquire and speculate in this way any more, and that if you are caught doing so again, you shall die;—if this was the condition on which you let me go, I should reply: Men of Athens, I honor and love you; but I shall obey God rather than you, and while I have life and strength I shall never cease from the practice and teaching of philosophy, exhorting anyone whom I meet and saying to him after my manner: You, my friend—a citizen of the great and mighty and wise city of Athens—are you not ashamed of heaping up the greatest amount of money and honor and reputation, and caring so little about wisdom and truth and the greatest improvement of the soul, which you never regard or heed at all? . . . For I do nothing but go about persuading you all, old and young alike, not to take thought for your persons or your properties, but first and chiefly to care about the greatest improvement of the soul."[13]

---
[13] Plato, *Apology*, 28f.

One of the latest estimates of the worth of Socrates to the world says among other things: "His significance for us lies in the fact that he is the first and most perfect example of the spirit of science—if science is the pursuit of truth for its own sake. He has the ideal of science; he used to say that there was only one good, knowledge, and only one evil, ignorance. He has its ardor, and at the age of seventy is still so keen in the pursuit of truth, that his last hours were given to it. He has its patience and caution: that is why his dialogues often end without a conclusion; for he would rather admit ignorance than accept an untested or unsatisfactory answer. He has its self-control and self-suppression, and never loses his temper in a discussion, is never discourteous or unfair. He has its courage, and is never frightened or shocked or irritated by any view, but always ready dispassionately to examine it. He has its perfect disinterestedness, and is ready to test his own opinions as well as those of others: for he remembered what disputants generally forget, his own ignorance and fallibility."[14]

In the Crito Socrates says, "It is wrong to requite injustice with injustice, or to inflict evil upon any man, whatever we may suffer

[14] Livingstone, *op. cit.*, pp. 273-274.

at his hand."[15] There is a sublimity in this morality to which the most of us have not yet attained. It is the morality of the Sermon on the Mount. Both Socrates and Jesus believed in it and realized it in their life and death. They would both of them despise the militarism of Europe, Asia, and America.

Professor Karl Joel, in his *Philosophenwege*, has written: "Let us imagine Socrates introduced in a dream into our times. Astonished, he would gaze at our wonderful means of transportation, the mass of factory products, the long-range guns, the luxurious comfort of our private houses, the crowded libraries, the splendor of the theaters—in a word, all the wealth of our age. 'Should we not be proud and happy?' we might ask him. In his characteristic manner he might answer, 'I cannot tell yet, as I am not acquainted with your modes of thought, and have not yet learned whether you are good and wise. Show me your living masters.' The next day in the Palestra Socrates would relate to his companions, 'I dreamed last night that I was in Persia. There everything is bigger than you can imagine. Enormously huge are the cities, the buildings, the treasures, the armies, the factories—everything gigantically big, nothing is

---
[15]Plato, *Crito* 49.

small, except the people.' "[16] We live as far below the Socratic ideal as most professing Christians live below the ideal set before them in the New Testament. The farther we stray from either ideal the worse it will be for the race.

There is another philosopher of Greece to whom the world always will feel immeasurably indebted. Plato was the pupil of Socrates. Aristotle was the pupil of Plato. He appeared at Plato's Academy when he was seventeen years of age, and for twenty years he studied there. When Plato died Aristotle was thirty-seven years old, and he went into retirement for five years to think his way through the accumulated learning of his twenty years in school. He summarized all the best products of Greek thought. He wrote the first encyclopedia, and he did all the work alone. For seven years he was the teacher and the mentor of Alexander the Great. For thirteen years the greatest school of the ancient world was conducted and maintained by him, and he made it a school for advanced philosophers.

He created the science of logic. No one knew its laws before him, and no one has added a law to the science since his day. Kant, the greatest of the modern philosophers, said,

---
[16]Martin, *op. cit.*, p. 124.

"Logic since Aristotle, like geometry since Euclid, is a finished science."[17] He gathered enormous accumulations of facts, and he insisted upon scientific methods in the investigation and classification of these facts. He formulated the scientific and philosophical vocabulary and gave it a definiteness which has been of incalculable benefit to all the succeeding generations. He wrote the history of thought.

He laid the foundations for most of the natural sciences, and Sir William Hamilton declares, "Aristotle's seal is upon all the sciences, his speculations have determined those of all subsequent thinkers." Hegel said, "Aristotle was a genius beside whom no age has an equal to place,"[18] and again, "Aristotle penetrated into the whole universe of things and subjected its scattered wealth to intelligence: to him the greater number of the philosophical sciences owe their origin and differentiation." Goethe agreed, "If I had my youthful faculties at command now, nature and Aristotle should be my sole study. It is beyond all conception what that man saw, remarked, observed."[19] He took all knowledge

---
[17]Martin, *op. cit.*, p. 37.
[18]*Ibid.*, p. 38.
[19]*Ibid.*

for his province. He made a science of biology. He believed all facts were worth knowing and systematizing. He extended the realms of investigation beyond mathematics and music and philosophy, and made the natural sciences equally respectable with their august predecessors.

This is the way he talked about natural knowledge in comparison with a knowledge of astronomy: "The glory, doubtless, of the heavenly bodies fills us with more delight than the contemplations of those lowly things; for the sun and stars are born not, neither do they decay, but are eternal and divine. But the heavens are high and afar off, and of celestial things the knowledge that our senses give us is scanty and dim. The living creatures, on the other hand, are at our door, and if we so desire it, we may gain ample and certain knowledge of each and all. We take pleasure in the beauty of a statue; shall not then the living fill us with delight, and all the more if in the spirit of philosophy we search for causes and recognize the evidences of design? Then will nature's purpose and her deep-seated laws be everywhere revealed, all tending in her multitudinous work to one form or another of the Beautiful." It is his apology for his temerity in introducing the natural

THE GREEK TESTAMENT 147

sciences into the company of philosophy and mathematics and astronomy, and it is an adequate apology.

The reign of law is as apparent in animal life as in astronomy. There is as much beauty and symmetry and accuracy in biology as in music and mathematics. The search for causes and the evidences of design is as rewarding in this field as in philosophy. Aristotle saw these things clearly and his researches and conclusions convinced all the after generations that he was right. His influence dominated the teachings of the schools for centuries.

Aristotle desired to know the cause of all results. He demanded the reason for everything. He was unwell at one time and was treated by a physician and the physician made a prescription and was about to leave it with him when Aristotle said, "Do not treat me as you would a country bumpkin. Give me a reason for your treatment and I will take it."[20] He was not willing to be cured by faith. He was willing to be cured only by reasonable treatment. No wonder that he has made such an abiding impression upon all cultured and reasoning minds.

Professor Romanes bears his testimony to

---
[20] Ælian, *Var. Hist.*, ix, 23.

the impression which Aristotle has made upon him in these words: "It appears to me that there can be no question that Aristotle stands forth not only as the greatest figure in antiquity, but as the greatest intellect that has ever appeared upon this earth."[21] Professor Hyslop adds suggestively, "Aristotle is the hero of those who ask no favors of the universe except to know the truth." Darwin wrote to a friend, "From quotations I had seen I had a high notion of Aristotle's merits, but I had not the most remote notion what a wonderful man he was. Linnæus and Cuvier have been my two gods, though in very different ways, but they were mere schoolboys to old Aristotle."

Aristotle wrote on agriculture and astronomy, anthropology and anatomy, biology and botany, optics and physics, meteorology and metaphysics, mathematics and mechanics, physiology and psychology, poetry and politics, rhetoric and logic, moral philosophy and zoology, and much of what he wrote was epoch-making and much of it is valid for our thought to-day. It was Coleridge who said that to this day every thinking man was either a Platonist or an Aristotelian. All thoughtful persons still read and study these great mas-

---
[21] Martin, *op. cit.*, p. 38.

ters of those who know. It was given to them to seek the truth with whole-hearted devotion, and it was given to them to know the truth as none before them had known it and as few if any since have mastered it.

It is to such fearless souls, and to such alone, that the truth is revealed. The revelation was poured out upon them without measure, and therefore, as Sidgwick in the *Outline of the History of Ethics* has said, it has come to pass that "in the general view of present scholarship, there is no moral philosopher of modern times, with the doubtful exception of Kant, who equals in importance and impressiveness Socrates, Plato, or Aristotle."[22]

They have had no successors in the world of thought and it is true that

"Every thought of all their thinking swayed the world for good or ill,
Every pulse of all their life-blood beats across the ages still."

One finds their impress on every modern work of note, and all modern culture acknowledges its dependence upon these three intellectual masters and pioneers.

We will read on through Herodotus, the most entertaining of historians, whose narra-

---
[22]Martin, *op. cit.*, p. 163.

tive Wordsworth thought was "the most interesting and instructive book, next to the Bible, which had ever been written." Then we will read through Thucydides, the tersest and most philosophical of historians, of whom Macaulay said: "This day I finished Thucydides, after reading him with inexpressible interest and admiration. He is the greatest historian that ever lived." Over a year later he made the record, "I am still of the same mind."

Thucydides is impartial in his judgments, as Herodotus was, and far more accurate than Herodotus claimed to be. He had the spirit of a scientist and the imagination of a poet. Livingstone says of him, "He feels the tragedy of his story, and divines beneath the hard facts of it the ideas that give them life and meaning. Yet he remains accurate, scientific, impartial. Such a union of truth and imagination is not to be found in Gibbon, Macaulay, Froude, or any other English historian. It is found in Thucydides, and that, no doubt, is why he has been called the greatest of historians. His History has the tragic quality of Shakespeare or Æschylus, yet the veracity of scientific work."[23] E. A. Freeman said of his work, "There is hardly a problem in the science of government which the statesman will not find

---
[23] Livingstone, *The Pageant of Greece*, p. 202.

THE GREEK TESTAMENT 151

handled, if not solved, in the pages of this universal master."[24] He remains an authority in the field of politics to-day.

We will read on to that greatest of orators and last great Athenian, Demosthenes, of whom Cicero said, "He alone towers above all men in every kind of oratory, so that no higher eloquence can be required." Bossuet calls the Oration for the Crown "the greatest work of the human mind."

We may not tarry longer, even to mention the works of Aristophanes, Pindar, Sappho, and Anacreon, or of any other of the great names of the Canon, though they will all repay close and continued study. It is a wonderful and magnificent literature, the literature of the Greeks. For more than two thousand years a knowledge of this language and literature has been deemed essential to culture. It never can be dethroned from its position of primacy among the literatures of the world. Professor Butcher was right when he called it "the one entirely original literature of Europe." It was not only first, but greatest. It includes the greatest poets, the greatest historians, the greatest orators, the greatest philosophers. Its achievements are of unrivaled importance to the race.

[24] Freeman, *Historical Essays*, second series, iii.

PART V

A WONDERFUL BOOK

THE GREATEST GREEK BOOK: THE NEW TESTAMENT

WHEN the Alexandrian Library had been completed and after the Alexandrian Canon had been established, only one book was to be added to this marvelous literature of the Greeks which would in any sense rival, equal, or surpass those which had gone before. Wonderful as the Greek literature was, one book was yet to be written which was to be more wonderful than any the Greeks yet had in its content and in its influence, and which will be loved and cherished forever as the final presentation of the perfect ideal. The New Testament of the Christian Church has been more widely read and always will be more highly valued than any other volume in the Greek tongue. It is the crowning glory of the Greek that in the fullness of time God made it his chosen language through which to transmit to the world the good news of the world's salvation.

THE GREEK TESTAMENT 153

The Hebrews were the chosen people, prepared through millenniums of history for the world's evangelization to the true faith. The Son of man came to this chosen people and confined his ministry strictly within its narrow boundaries and much of his teaching to its Aramaic tongue. The twelve apostles were all Hebrews, as was the great apostle to the Gentiles, Paul. All the authors of the books in our New Testament canon, with the possible exception of Luke, who may have been a Gentile, were of the Hebrew race. Some of the books of the New Testament, as the Gospel according to Matthew and the Epistle to the Hebrews, seem designed especially for the Hebrews among the early Christians. One of the Epistles was written for the church in the city of Rome and one for the Gauls in Asia Minor. Yet all the Gospels and Epistles were written in Greek, and the whole of our New Testament revelation from the first Epistle of Paul to the last Epistle of John was intrusted to this chosen and preeminent tongue.

The Old Testament had been translated into Greek some two centuries before, at Alexandria, which was the first great meetingplace of the Hebrew scholarship and the Greek culture. Mahaffy declares, "By far the greatest contribution of Alexandrian prose to the great literature of the world is this very translation of the Old Testament." It was "the first apostle to the Gentiles," introducing the sacred literature of the Jews to the other peoples, and it was the only Bible known to most of the Jews in the world in the time of Jesus. The names "Christ," "Christian," and "Christianity" came out of this book. The first complete Bible was the Greek Bible, a Greek New Testament being added to the Greek Old Testament to make it.

Most of the authorities agree that Jesus and his apostles could understand, read, and speak Greek, and the Greek translation of the Holy Scriptures became the Bible of their common and daily use. In thirty-three out of thirty-seven passages in which Jesus referred to the Old Testament he quotes from the Septuagint. Of three hundred and fifty quotations in the New Testament three hundred are from the Greek and not from the Hebrew. The Greek language was in a measure regenerated by the Christian spirit which took possession of it; but the Christian movement appropriated the Greek tongue partly because of convenience and necessity and largely because it was the richest and most beautiful language men ever had made, and thus in Divine Providence it was chosen as the fittest

THE GREEK TESTAMENT 155

medium for the preservation of the Gospel among men. The Old Testament was translated into Greek; the New Testament was written in Greek; the Pentecostal gift of tongues covered the various dialects of the Greek; all Christian literature for some centuries was Greek and only Greek.

Professor Briggs has said, "There are no languages, not even the English and the German, which could so adequately convey the divine revelation in its simplicity, grandeur, fullness, variety, energy and impressiveness as those selected by Divine Providence for the purpose."[1] McClymont avers, "The Greek was marvelously fitted for this purpose, on account of its unrivaled clearness, richness, and flexibility."[2] No language before it, said Professor Townsend, had been "so eminently adapted for enshrining and transmitting ordinary facts and spiritual truths." "As the most beautiful, rich, and harmonious language ever spoken and written," says Philip Schaff, it was worthy to "form the pictures of silver in which the golden apple of the gospel should be preserved for all generations."[3]

[1] Briggs, *The Study of Holy Scripture*, p. 43.
[2] McClymont, *The New Testament and Its Writers*, p. 2.
[3] Schaff, *History of the Apostolic Church*, p. 145. Charles Scribner's Sons. Used by permission.

The language of Homer and Plato, of Herodotus and Demosthenes, of Æschylus and Aristotle was the divinely chosen language for the record of the words and the works of the Christ. One more book was to be added to this wonderful literature of the Greeks, surpassing all the rest; one last swan-song of this classic tongue, a song of supernatural melody entrancing all souls—the New Testament revelation bringing life and immortality to light. The Greek New Testament, though written by Jews, is the one invaluable volume in the Greek tongue, and the most important book in the world's literature.

It claims to contain the record of the clearest, fullest, crowning revelation of God to man. It has to do with the highest interests of the human soul. It deals with the supremest concern of the race. It comes out of the heart of the Hebrew nation, a people divinely disciplined through the centuries to be a religious people, worthy worshipers of the one true God in distinction from the heathen everywhere. The oracles of God, the sacred books revealing God's being and will, had been intrusted to them; and now, as the flower of the series, closing the canon of their inspired literature, the most beautiful language in the world was pressed into the service of

THE GREEK TESTAMENT 157

this fulfillment and consummation of the Hebrew faith; and the New Testament revelation was written by Hebrew authors in Greek. The Hellenic tongue was made "the vehicle of higher truths and a holier inspiration than had ever haunted the dreams of bard or sage in old Achaia."

The Greek New Testament is a little book, but it is the greatest and best of all books. Dean Stanley was visiting Ewald at Dresden and in the course of the conversation Ewald snatched up a copy of the Greek New Testament which was lying on the table at his side and said in his usual impulsive way, "In this little book is contained all the wisdom of the world." He was right. The little volume contains the highest, clearest, fullest revelation of the truth that men ever have known; and it is the most precious book on the earth to-day. If all books were to be destroyed and we were given the privilege of choosing one book, and only one, which could be saved from the general wreck, of course we would choose the Bible; and if all the Bible could not be preserved, we would ask for the New Testament, and of course we would ask for the New Testament in a critical edition of the Greek. If our library were to be limited to a single volume, this is the volume we would choose.

Surely every Christian would make the same choice.

Self-evidently the Greek New Testament would be of small service to one to whom the language would be unfamiliar. So that our former proposition would resolve itself into this, that every Christian, realizing the incomparable importance of the Greek New Testament, surely would avail himself of any and every opportunity to make himself acquainted with New Testament Greek. The Greek New Testament is the real New Testament. An English New Testament is only a translation of the original and genuine and real New Testament, and whoever would have first-hand authority in the New Testament must be able to read it in the original for himself.

The sad fact of the case is that a large majority of Christians are not able to do that; and yet the acquisition of New Testament Greek is desirable for and possible to all. College advantages are not necessary in these days to one who is really desirous of carrying on the study of Greek. New Testament Greek is comparatively simple and easy Greek, and it does not need any advanced course or long study to read it. It is our opinion that any average student who will find one hour a day to put into faithful work on his Greek can begin in absolute ignorance of the grammar and language and in three years' time can read with relative ease the whole of the New Testament. One hour a day for three years, or even less than that.

Some years ago a young wife became ambitious to read and study Greek. She had not studied the language in college. She was set to work on the Greek grammar. She did not like it. It is very rarely that any student does. She could not put more time upon it than one hour a day. So all one year through she got no farther than the Grammar and Greek Prose Composition; but at the end of the year she began to read the Anabasis. In one week she was interested as she had not been before. In two months she had read the whole of the Anabasis, the seven books (students usually read only four in school), and she had read them without any translation or help, reciting each day with moods and tenses, persons and numbers accurately rendered and translation literal and absolutely correct. Then she began the New Testament, and read it through twice; and after a year and a half, when her ability to read at sight was put to the test, she read a chapter without the lexicon, needing help on but five or six words. She said she would have been willing to study three years instead of one year for the pleasure she had had in her reading in those three months. What she did, others can do. To be sure, she was a brilliant student, but she had many claims upon her time and attention in that year and a half in which she began the study of Greek, doing her housework and taking care of her baby; and in double that time, in three years, we have no doubt that any average mind can do all that she did.

To read Greek one must know something of Greek grammar and prose composition, and that means hard work in the beginning. "The first study of the language is as dry and uninteresting as anything possibly can be. It is drill, drill, drill, forms, forms, forms, rules, rules, rules, conjugations and declensions, patient and long-continued memorizing, almost a desert of disjointed facts." Yet beyond the desert lies Arabia, the land of the blest. It took long climbing and hard fighting to get up the Heights of Abraham, but only a few days later the whole fair city of Quebec was in the possession of the faithful and tireless climbers. The rock of Gibraltar seemed well-nigh impregnable, and Sir George Rooke and his soldiers had hard work to scale it; but, once mounted and mastered, there was

THE GREEK TESTAMENT 161

smooth sailing thereafter over all the blue Mediterranean beyond.

No one denies that the study of Greek in the beginning is hard; but hear what Hesiod, an old Greek writer, once said: "It is possible to seize upon worthless things easily and in heaps: for the path to them is plain and lies very near. But the immortal gods have placed sweat before every worthy achievement: afar and steep is the road that leads to it and rough at first. But when one comes to the height then truly is it easy, though so hard before."[4] The study of Greek at first is hard; but hear what Epicharmus, another Greek writer, once said, "The gods sell all good things to us for toil," and remember what Sophocles has written, "No one, being lazy, gains anything good; but toils, and toils alone, beget great glory," and again, "Labor having been left behind, labors are sweet." That is to say, when the hard work is once done, the harvest is an ample reward for all toil.

It is well worth while to learn something about Greek grammar because all such knowledge will help us to understand more of our Greek New Testament. Luther once said, "The science of theology is nothing else than grammar exercised on the words of the Holy

[4]Hesiod, O. D., 287ff.

Spirit." Possibly that statement, like so many others made by that impetuous German soul, may seem a little extravagant; but all will agree that Joseph Agar Beet is well within the limits of the truth when he says: "No one who earnestly desires to learn all he can from the Bible and who, with this aim in view, strives to follow the train of thought of its writers, will count any labor superfluous which enables him to understand more exactly and fully the meaning of their words. The sense which lies on the surface of Scripture is often very far from the correct one. And our chief aid in discovering the true sense is accurate grammatical analysis. Much oftener than is commonly supposed have grammatical mistakes given rise to errors in doctrine. And still more frequently have the clearer views obtained by grammatical study borne fruit in the spiritual life of the student."[5]

Fairbairn used to say that he is no theologian who is not first a grammarian; and the same thing is true of anyone who attempts to give an adequate exposition of any portion of the Scripture. Grammar may become a direct aid to grace. The diligent student of his Greek Testament will grow in grace while his neighbor who knows no Greek and is content

[5] Expositor, 1881, pp. 384-385.

THE GREEK TESTAMENT 163

with his English becomes more and more a disgrace in his efforts at interpretation of the Word whose deepest secrets are hidden in its original tongue.

Some people may think that it is a great pity that the knowledge of Greek cannot be granted by the imposition of hands; but neither the gift of tongues nor the gift of interpretation can be bestowed in that manner. Very possibly there would be no advantage in that arrangement. The gift might be bestowed only upon certain favorites or its acquisition might be purchasable with money and thus become the property only of the well-to-do, while now it is open to all. Then the Greek handed down in an apostolical succession by the imposition of hands might come under the same suspicion with the grace handed down in that way, and there might be reason to think that it had become rather thin in quality during the course of its transmission, or indeed that it had disappeared entirely.

There is no royal road to the knowledge of Greek. What Horace said about all valuable learning is applicable here: "He who would excel must first toil long . . . and tremble before the schoolmaster." Grace may be as free as the sunshine and the air; but Greek does not come to a man as easily as breathing. Too many men get their theology from the atmosphere of the times in which they live. They bask in current beliefs as in the sunshine. They breathe in the current dogmas and the popular fads as if they were the adequate and final sources of inspiration. Paul intimates that the deep things of God are to be found by searching.[6] The man who does not search for them in the original tongues is likely to depend upon his own cleverness or his own dullness and to find out to his sorrow that his thoughts are not God's thoughts in many instances.

We must go to this original to find the "perpetual remainders of precious truth left untranslated" because no two languages are exactly commensurate and it is impossible for the English completely to reproduce the Greek. The single words of one language never can represent the single words of another language. The idioms of one language never are the exact equivalents of the idioms of another language. Of necessity all translations are only approximations. To get at the original truth the translation must be supplemented by paraphrase and exposition, and these are accurately possible only to the reader of the original tongues.

---

[6] 1 Cor. 2. 10.

THE GREEK TESTAMENT 165

One of the most recent translators of the New Testament apologizes for the imperfection of his work, scholarly and able as it is, and then says, "To translate from one language into another is like playing on the piano what was written for the violin. The fundamental melody may be faithfully reproduced, but many subtle effects which the composer intended are inevitably lost, and effects which he did not intend are added."[7] Another authority declares, "It is said that we may know the classics through translations. That is either sophistry or ignorance. We may recognize them, but we shall never know them. Who can copy the Aphrodite of Melos or a painting by Raphael so that his work will have half the value of the original? Yet such work may be much nearer to reproduction than any translation of a great author can be."[8]

Surely, then, anyone who is responsible for the exposition of the Scriptures ought to know the words and the idioms of the original. He comes somewhere short of the fullness of the truth contained in them when he does not know them. In one of the series of Yale Lectures on Preaching, and in one of the best in

---

[7] Ballentine, *The Riverside New Testament*, p. vi. Houghton Mifflin Company. Used by permission.
[8] D. O. S. Lowell, in West, *op. cit.*, p. 199.

that series, the lecturer took for one of his subjects "Veracity in Ministers," and under that head he exhorted to a faithful philological and exegetical study of the original tongues, as absolutely necessary to their truthfulness. He put his point very strongly: "I say to you to-day it is a matter of integrity also. What is slander? Well, one form of it is reporting that a man said something that he did not say. And why is not the Bible slandered when some inaccurate and unexegetical fumbler spends several hours every week in public discoursings on what the Bible says?

"Unquestionably the Bible does say many things that he declares it does. The general tone of its teachings on the principal topics of doctrine and life, he gets at. But the Bible is like a person. It has in it, so to speak, virgin-like and elusive qualities and shades of quality which must be perceived in order to a complete and completely relishable acquaintance with the book. A merely English scholar may get a good deal from the Bible; but a Greek and Hebrew scholar can get more. Words fairly quiver with delight when you hunt them out clear to their radicals. . . . It is impossible to get the whole marrow of Greek or Hebrew or Latin thought in an English rendering of it. Hebrew thought in an

English dress is Anglicized-Hebrew thought always—more or less.

"Thought, that essence of the mind, instinctively takes on a body of language that is surcharged with its own idiosyncrasies, and any other embodiment would be a misfit to a degree and so far not an embodiment. . . . So then our very veracity forces us to philology, to exegesis, to profound interpretation. If we intentionally misrepresent meanings, we are liars, plain as day. But if we misrepresent meanings through carelessness, or through laziness, it shows that we have in us the making of a liar. We are willing to make statement after statement that we never have taken the trouble to verify. We are leaving a large part of the significance of our Bible—many a savory term, phrase, turn and idiom—unused and undetected."[9]

It is difficult to convince the man without experience in translating that the translation in his hand is not good enough for all purposes. He is ready to say: "What is the use of my spending time and labor in learning how to read the New Testament in Greek, when I have it already in the King James Version and the Revised Versions, translated most admira-

[9]Burton, *In Pulpit and Parish*, pp. 340-341. Congregational Publishing Society. Used by permission.

bly into elegant English? Are not these translations as good as the Greek?" We answer most emphatically, "No!"—and it may be well to insist a little on this point.

Matthew, Mark, and Luke, Peter and Paul, James and John and Jesus and Jude did not know English. The only way to converse with these men on familiar terms is to know their language and to hear them speak their own tongue; and, in the fullness of their content, no man ever began to know all that Jesus has said and the apostles have written until he knew the words they used and the thought which lay in them. One would think that this did not need the saying; but you never can tell. One of my colleagues was lecturing, and having invited questions at the close of the talk, a good sister on the front row immediately put to him this poser: "You say that the apostles were unlearned men. How, then, do you explain the fact that they used such good grammar and spoke such good English?" They did not speak English. There in the Wartburg Luther lamented, "It is so hard to make these Hebrew prophets speak German!" It is equally hard and at many points it is impossible to make the Christian apostles speak English.

Our English translations are good; but all

THE GREEK TESTAMENT 169

translations must in the very nature of things be defective to a serious degree, since every language has its peculiarities which belong to itself alone and which cannot be reproduced in any other. Miss Swanwick's translation of Faust is considered by many critics to be a very masterpiece of its kind, and yet he who would most thoroughly enjoy the greatest poem of the greatest German poet must read it in the original German, Goethe's native tongue. No English translation can give the finer shades of thought, the more delicate felicities of expression, the deeper beauties of meaning which the original language affords. What is true of the German is true of any other tongue. "Shakespeare would not be Shakespeare in Latin. Tennyson would hardly be recognizable in French. Webster's orations could not be made to thunder in Italian." "There never yet was a translation which did not leave much untranslated, because untranslatable."

The Greek student, therefore, with his Greek Testament in his hand, reading the very words written or spoken by the apostles Peter or Paul, comes more nearly to the men themselves and to their meaning than anyone can hope to with an English version; for he reads the teaching or hears the preaching of the men themselves, while the student of the translation reads that teaching or hears that preaching through an interpreter. Possibly we could have no better interpreters than the King James and the Revised Versions are, but yet it remains true that the English language in our English Bibles is but an interpreter still. An interpreter may give us the general sense of a passage, but he cannot give us the shading. He may give us a faint or a full reflection of the truth, but he cannot reproduce for us the living image of the original.

We remember that sentence in the Great Sermon, "Verily I say unto you, till heaven and earth pass away, one jot or one tittle [one iota or one keraia]¹⁰ shall in no wise pass away from the law, till all things be accomplished."¹¹ What does that phrase, "one jot or one tittle, one iota or one keraia," mean, unless it be that even the smallest portions, the seemingly most unimportant parts, are radically significant and essentially important in gospel evolution and the Kingdom's consummation? There is nothing unimportant, not even the jots and the tittles, in the revelation from God. We remember also what Jesus went on immediately to say, "Whosoever

---

[10] ἰῶτα ἓν ἢ μία κερέα.
[11] Matt. 5. 18.

therefore shall break one of these least portions of the commandments, and shall teach men so, shall be called least in the kingdom of heaven: but whosoever shall do and teach them, he shall be called great in the kingdom of heaven."[12] We make the statement without fear of contradiction or question that the Christian who is unacquainted with the original Greek misses countless multitudes of these jots and tittles of the written record and law, and therefore is in great danger of teaching men amiss in some one or other of these lesser points or least portions; and he who does so when he has the opportunity to know the whole truth and preach it, is in danger of the judgment here pronounced by the Christ.

"There are in every New Testament book," says Professor Buell, "fervors, sighs, hearttones, tears half discernible, laughter unmistakable, plays upon words, deft and delicate railleries and ironies, the impress of which the Greek tongue, plastic as Pompeian ashes, has preserved. Translate them? Well, yes, when you can dig the fly out of the amber, and write out on paper the song of the sky-lark!" Jots and tittles—trifles, did we call them? "They are trifles, but yet in the same sense in which the artist's last minute

[12]Matt. 5. 19.

dot of white paint in the eye of his all-but-finished portrait is a trifle. We know it is that which lends to the eye its evanescent but characteristic sparkle, and such a true token of lifelikeness, however unobtrusive, is no trifle."

Possibly it may be well to illustrate and prove some of these statements. We say that the Greek language has peculiarities which are untranslatable. Let us notice a few of these.

I. First, some of its words are peculiar to itself, and have no equivalent in English. For example, we were reading in the college class in Demosthenes and came to the phrase ὕπουλον ἡσυχίαν, which we translated "hollow silence," a very awkward English phrase and a wholly inadequate translation, but the best we could do with our English. In the Edinburgh Review a critic says, "How far this translation falls short of the original will be seen when, in order to express the literal meaning of that single word ὕπουλον we are of necessity driven to this periphrasis—a hollow silence like that particular state of a wound which has just skinned over, as if about to heal, but which is nevertheless rankling underneath and just upon the point of breaking out into fresh mischief." All of the meaning is in the single word in the Greek, but no translator would

THE GREEK TESTAMENT 173

think of stopping to give it; and yet the whole meaning is essential to the adequate conception of the picture presented by Demosthenes.

How often the translations in the New Testament are likewise inadequate.

1. John records the words of the Lord, "In my Father's house are many mansions."[13] The Greek word is μοναί, formed upon the Greek verb μένω as its root; and why our English versions should translate it "mansions" is more than we can tell. We know of course that the word "mansions" came into our versions from the Latin version in the Vulgate, "mansiones"; but why that mistranslation of the Latin should have been carried over into the English and maintained there, we cannot see. The Greek word means "abiding-places, resting-places"; the very heart of our English word "home" is in it. The same word occurs in the twenty-third verse of this fourteenth chapter of the Gospel according to John, "If any one love me, he will keep my word, and my Father will love him, and we will come to him—and we will stay! We will come to him, and we will abide! We will make our abode with him. We will make his heart our abiding-place, our resting-place, our home!"[14]

---
[13] John 14. 2.
[14] John 14. 23, καὶ μονὴν παρ αὐτῷ ποιησόμεθα.

Mansions! there is no thought of mansions in that word, no least suggestion of magnificence or stateliness or coldness or liveried servants or painful formality. It is just the plain, simple, hearty, wholesome word for Home. Here in the second verse Jesus meant to say: "You always are glad to get back to the Father's house, the old home. You enjoy going into the parlor where there have been so many pleasant calls from your friends. You enjoy the old sitting room, where with father and mother, brothers and sisters, the whole family gathered at night about the fire. You enjoy the dining room where day after day you thanked God for his bounty, and cheerful conversation gave you heart for your work. Yet you love most of all that little room that stands apart, the room that was all your own, sacred to your retirement and rest. There the throbbing head began to cool; and the heart struggle was quieted. It was your refuge, your resting place, your retreat. When you turned the key in the door there, and the whole surging world was locked outside, there you were at peace." Jesus meant to say, and he did say, "Let not your heart be troubled. In my Father's house are many resting-places, just like that," and the reader of the Greek Testament sees that meaning at the very first

THE GREEK TESTAMENT 175

glance. The student of the English version merely never gets it at all.

These inadequate translations occur everywhere in the New Testament and they are unavoidable because the Greek peculiarities cannot be paralleled in the English.

2. Take that passage, Rom. 3. 2, 3, for an example. One Greek root is four times repeated there, and the student of the Greek recognizes that fact at once and has it in mind in his interpretation and translation. What did the Authorized Version do in that passage? It translated the four occurrences of that single root by four different words, and the reader of the English only never might have suspected that there was any etymological connection between them. It read, "Unto them were committed the oracles of God. For what if some did not believe? Shall their unbelief make the faith of God without effect?" Committed, believe, unbelief, faith; who would have suspected that those four words went back to the same root in the Greek?

The Revised Version does better when it says, "They were intrusted with the oracles of God. For what if some of them were without faith? shall their want of faith make of none effect the faithfulness of God?" Yet here we still have three words to express the meaning of that one Greek root. We cannot translate its meaning into English without considerable circumlocution, such as our versions cannot employ. The play on words in the Greek might be suggested in the English by a paraphrase like this: "The oracles of God were committed to them as trustworthy depositories who would faithfully obey them. For what if some proved untrustworthy and disobedient? shall their breach of trust make God untrustworthy in his promises and purposes concerning Israel?" This is the translation of Howard Crosby and it has the merit of reproducing something at least of the Greek play on words in the English; but it is more of a paraphrase than a translation.

All the meaning of the paraphrase is apparent to the student of the original as soon as he looks at the Greek. It never is suspected by most of the readers of the English.

3. Then there are words which have double meanings in the Greek, like the word "Logos," which means both "Reason" and "Word" and is not satisfactorily translated by either alone, and the word "Paraclete," which is translated both "Comforter" and "Advocate" in our versions, although neither of those terms is an adequate translation in any passage.

THE GREEK TESTAMENT 177

In the Methodist Magazine for 1803 there is the funeral sermon of Christopher Hopper, one of the most faithful of Wesley's early preachers. In that sermon this paragraph occurs: "As he considered the Scriptures of the Old and New Testament to be of the utmost importance, both to himself and to mankind at large, and believing it impossible for them to be translated into foreign languages without depriving them of their native beauties, he regarded it a duty which he owed to himself, to God, and the church to acquire some knowledge of those languages in which the Scriptures were originally written." One would think that a conviction of the same truths would lead to the same conclusion on the part of any earnest Christian.

4. Take that passage found in the Epistle of James, "Every good gift and every perfect gift is from above, and cometh down from the Father of lights, with whom is no variableness, neither shadow of turning."[15] So it read in the Authorized Version; and the reader of the English of those last two clauses might have gathered the comforting truth that God was not subject to any slightest variation or change, but that would be about all he could extract from that translation. We say that a

---
[15] Jas. 1. 17.

prisoner has no shadow of a chance to escape, and we mean that he has no chance at all. We say that there is no shadow of hope for his deliverance, and we mean that there is no hope at all. Then when we say that with God there is no shadow of turning do we mean that there is no slightest or least turning, no turning at all? Probably many an English reader of this passage has supposed that that was its meaning.

The Revised Version helped us at that point when it translated, "the Father of lights, with whom there can be no variation, neither shadow that is cast by turning." At least that translation makes it perfectly clear that the "shadow" of the original is a literal shadow and that the word is not to be interpreted figuratively. However, the Greek reads, παρ᾽ ᾧ οὐκ ἔνι παραλλαγὴ ἢ τροπῆς ἀποσκίασμα, and the fullness of meaning in the Greek phrases can be made apparent only in an exposition and not in any translation.

The reader of the Greek perceives at the first glance that James has introduced an astronomical figure here, and that he represents God as the Father of lights, and nothing but lights, sending forth light at all times and into all places and never sending forth a shadow anywhere; like the sun in the zenith,

THE GREEK TESTAMENT   179

casting no shadow in any direction; only that God is everywhere and his zenith is everywhere. He sees things as they are with no shadows upon them. He knows things as they are. He knows what really good and perfect gifts will be. The sun changes its position continually; but that is not true of the Father of lights. The moon has the shadow of the earth cast upon it occasionally; but no shadow ever falls upon him. He sees all, and he sees all alike. All may see him, always the same. There is no shadow upon him to our gaze. The conception of the unchanging God which our English versions gave us is indefinitely enriched when we turn to the untranslatable Greek.

5. In the Authorized Version of John 8. 30 we read, "As he spake these words many believed on him," and in the next following words we read, "Then said Jesus to those Jews which believed on him," and the reader of those English sentences in all probability never would suspect that there was a difference in the construction in the Greek which indicated that the believers of verse 30 were genuine believers, giving to Jesus the allegiance of their whole lives and hearts, while the believers of verse 31 were only believers in the teaching power of Jesus and were ready to antagonize

him and to accuse him of being possessed of a demon and to stone him to death. The Greek suggests that the belief in the two cases was radically different the one from the other, while the English translation never hinted it.

The Revised Version gave us a hint in the matter by omitting the preposition in verse 31 and translating, "those Jews which had believed him," but not one reader in a hundred of the English versions alone would know that in the Greek of verse 30 we had a new Greek construction to indicate the new experience of Christian faith and discipleship, unclassical and untranslatable while perfectly apparent to the student of the original. We are told that an old writer called the prepositions in New Testament Greek "montes doctrinarum," "mountains of theological importance," and we recall that Luther said, "There is a great divinity in prepositions," and there is no clearer example of this truth than in the prepositions which have to do with the Christian faith and life.

II. Another untranslatable peculiarity of the Greek is that its verbs very frequently compound themselves with many different prepositions, any one of which when used gives to the verb its own somewhat new or entirely different shade of meaning. Our English verbs cannot reproduce these varying meanings, since they cannot be similarly compounded.

1. For example, in Heb. 12. 2 we have that phrase, "looking unto Jesus," the author and finisher of our faith. The verb in the Greek is not the simple verb for "looking," ὁρῶντες, but the compound with the preposition ἀπό, ἀφορῶντες. This word, according to Thayer, means "turning the eyes away from other things and then fixing them upon something or someone." How much fuller that meaning than the one the English version gives! The writer of the Epistle to the Hebrews meant to say and did say, "You must look away from the cross, away from the shame, away from even the cloud of witnesses, away from everything which would either distract your attention or disturb your faith; and then, you must fix your eyes upon Jesus. Looking away from all other things, you must look to him alone." The student of the English New Testament alone gets only half of what the author of the epistle intended to say.

2. The verb τρέπω in the Greek means "to turn," and in the middle voice it means, "to turn oneself around." In 1 Cor. 4. 14 and in Heb. 12. 9 we find that verb compounded with the little preposition ἐν, meaning "in." In the former passage we translate, "I write not

these things to shame you," and in the latter passage we translate, "We gave our fathers reverence." Well, those are translations; but they give absolutely no hint of the fullness of the conception, the lifelikeness of the picture, expressed in the compound verb of the Greek. The Greek student as soon as he sees that word has in his mind's eye the vision of the sense of shame as something inside of one which causes him to turn his face away, hiding it in sheer mortification and disgrace; and he sees that to the Greek mind the sense of reverence and admiration was something inside of a man which made him turn about to look at or after the person he reverenced or admired.

3. In Rom. 8. 19 we read, "For the earnest expectation of the creation waiteth for the revealing of the sons of God." Expectation! That does not begin to express the picture in the Greek compound word. A recent English writer has suggested that the compound expresses the physical manifestation of eager expectancy in the head bent forward to catch the first glimpse of an advancing pageant or procession in the street. Then he employs another figure and says, "One finds oneself on a railway platform bending forward to get the first view of the oncoming engine, as it

THE GREEK TESTAMENT 183

rounds the edge of a curve which shortens the vision of the line. This is ἀποκαραδοκία, the expectancy of the outstretched head."[16] That is accurate but rather prosy. It can be put more poetically than that.

Godet, the eminent French commentator and accurate student of the Greek, says of this passage, "The Greek term which we translate by the word 'expectation' is one of those admirable words which the Greek language easily forms. It is composed of three elements, κάρα, 'the head'; δοκέω, δοκάω, δοκεύω, 'to wait for,' 'espy'; and ἀπό, 'from, from afar': so that the word ἀποκαραδοκία means, 'to wait with the head raised, and the eye fixed on that point of the horizon from which the expected object is to come.' What a plastic representation! An artist might make a statue of hope out of that Greek term." Yet in the English we have only that passive word, "expectation"; and we miss all the living energy in the Greek.

3. "The verb in this same sentence in Romans, ἀπεκδέχεται, which we translate 'waitcth for,' is not less remarkable: it is composed of the simple verb δέχομαι, 'to receive,' and the two prepositions, ἐκ, 'out of the hands of,' and ἀπό, 'from, from afar': so it means, 'to receive something from the hands of one who extends

[16] *Expository Times*, vol. xxii, p. 71.

it to you from afar.'" Put that Greek verb and substantive together and you have the picture of the suffering, sin-cursed creation, standing on tiptoe as it were, and looking eagerly out through the ages toward the dim horizon of Time for the first faint token of the Day-dawn of its deliverance, and stretching out its weary, empty hands in uttermost reach toward Him who some time will hand down from his faraway throne the ransom all-sufficient to redeem; but that picture comes altogether out of the Greek; and not at all from that insipid translation, "expectation," which simply sits down and folds its hands and "waits for" the revealing which is to come.

4. In the twenty-sixth verse of this same chapter in Romans we read, "And in like manner the Spirit also helpeth our infirmity." In the Greek the compound verb in this sentence is very expressive. It occurs in only one other passage in our New Testament, in the story of Martha and Mary. Jesus and his disciples had arrived, unexpectedly in all probability, at the Bethany home. Martha, as the responsible head of the household economy, was naturally much excited at the advent of such an imposing array of guests. Her hospitable soul was moved to strenuous exertion in their behalf. When they had been seated and told to

make themselves comfortable, she hurried away to prepare the rooms for their night lodging and to get the supper ready at once. There were thirteen hungry men to be provided for, and that meant a great deal of work. It was enough to tax any household's resources, and to tax any housewife's nervous energy.

Martha got along very well at first. She lit the fire and put the things on to cook. Then she got the bedrooms in order, and brought the water from the well. Then she carried out the benches and arranged the cushions on them for the company to recline comfortably at the evening meal. These benches were almost too heavy for one woman to carry; but she managed to do it alone. It was very warm weather and Martha was getting more and more tired. She was glad to have these people in her house, and she was glad to do all of these things for them; but there is a limit to any one's strength, and Martha had just about reached the limit. The whole burden of the entertainment had fallen upon her, and it weighed more and more heavily as the minutes flew by. Martha was cumbered about much serving. At last she tried to lift and push the heavy table into its place, and it was too much for her. She lifted and lifted, and though the table did not move, it almost broke her back.

186 GREEK CULTURE AND

Where was Mary all this time? Why was she not here to help? It was absolutely necessary to have another pair of hands at this juncture. Martha went in search of Mary and found her sitting at Jesus' feet. She was very cool and she looked very sweet, and Martha was very warm and very tired. There was just a touch of vexation in her tone, as she said, "Lord, is it no manner of care to thee that my sister was leaving me all this time to serve alone? Speak to her therefore that she may help me."[17]

"Help"? So we translate in our versions; but, help how, help in what way? Why, "Help me by taking hold of the other end of this heavy table and lifting it at the same time with me. The two of us can move it; but it is entirely too heavy for me to manage alone." How do we know that that was the kind of help which Martha needed? It is all expressed in the compound verb in the Greek. We have the simple verb compounded with two prepositions: λαμβάνω, "to take hold of," σύν, "together with," and ἀντί, "on the opposite side, over against." "Speak to her that she may συναντιλάβηται, that she may take hold of this heavy table at the same time that I do, together with me, and on the opposite side, over

[17] Luke 10. 40.

against me, so that the two of us can lift it into its proper place." That whole picture is there in the Greek verb, and it is wholly lost in the English translation "help," which might mean help of any sort and which does mean to the English reader everything in general and nothing in particular. Of course we may have imagined the wrong application of the picture; but the picture is there in the Greek as it is not in the English.

Now, to come back to our passage in Romans. This particular compound verb occurs in only these two passages in the New Testament.[18] In Romans we read, "In like manner the Spirit also helpeth our infirmities." He takes hold at the same time with us and lifts over against us until by our united effort the heaviest burden begins to move. "For we know not how to pray as we ought; but the Spirit maketh intercession for us with groanings which cannot be uttered." Maketh intercession; there is another picture verb in the Greek, another compound with three elements, the simple verb and two prepositions, τυγχάνω, to happen, ἐν, in, and ὑπέρ, in behalf of, ὑπερεντυγχάνει, to happen in, in just the nick of time, and ready and willing to assist.

Have we never been lifting at a heavy bur-

---
[18]Luke 10. 40 and Rom. 8. 26.

den which seemed too much for our strength and which would be so easy for two, and just when we were exhausted and ready to give up in despair, have we never been overjoyed to have a friend or neighbor happen along and lend us a willing hand till with his fresh vigor the task was easily done? There is the picture in that peculiar Greek verb, found nowhere else in the New Testament and nowhere in the Septuagint and nowhere in the classical Greek authors. The apostle Paul has coined this new word, it would seem, to fit the exigencies of his theme.

He says that prayer is no trivial thing. Prayer is the lever which lifts the flood-gates through which Omnipotence rushes down to our aid. All things are possible to prayer. According to our faith it shall be unto us; but so often our faith is so feeble and our prayers are so weak. We tug away at the lever, but the flood-gates are not lifted. Omnipotence does not come down in answer to our cry. At such times let no man give up in despair, says the apostle; for the Spirit is our Friend, and he has promised to happen in when we need him; and if we know not how to pray as we ought, if we are too weak to lift the lever alone, he will take hold on the other side, just opposite us, and he will lift at the same time that

THE GREEK TESTAMENT 189

we do; he will intercede together with us and for us with groanings that cannot be uttered, and what seemed impossible to our strength alone will be easy of accomplishment when he has come to our aid. Paul says all of that in the use of those two rather unusual compound verbs, and the force of neither of those verbs is in any measure adequately represented in the English. To translate those verbs completely is to furnish the adequate commentary on the passage; and the Greek student has it all at the first glance at the Greek words themselves.

The longer we live the more we appreciate the truth of what our professor of New Testament Greek once said: "The reading of the original is sometimes, as compared with the reading of commentaries, an economy of time and strength. What the commentator attempts to explain in many words and long periphrases, the Greek itself often flashes directly and graphically upon the mind. Indeed, it may be said that the tersest, wisest, most spiritual and most inspiring of commentaries on the New Testament in English is—the New Testament in Greek." We are reminded of that old Scotch woman, life-long student of the Word, to whom her pastor loaned some commentaries. She returned them after a time, saying, "They are good books. I find that the Bible throws much light upon them." The Greek New Testament throws much light upon the meaning of the Word, and light not found in the commentaries many times and not to be expected, because impossible, in an English translation.

It may be well to remark too at this point that all of the critical commentaries are based upon the original text, and it is almost impossible to use them without a knowledge of the Greek. They represent the accumulated results of centuries of research, and their aid frequently is indispensable and invaluable; but the reader without a knowledge of Greek finds himself barred from the use of all this rich treasure, because he stumbles over some Greek word or some Greek phrase in every paragraph or in every sentence which furnishes the indispensable clue to the whole discussion. We need the Greek Testament to understand the revelation. We need the Greek Testament to understand the best commentaries upon it.

We probably have said enough to prove that there are peculiarities in the Greek which are untranslatable into English and which are very important to one who would know the real and full meaning of the Word as first

THE GREEK TESTAMENT 191

spoken and written. There are other whole classes of peculiarities which we have not yet noticed.

III. The Greek has an abundance of little words called particles, "which answered to the play of feature or tone of voice in talking." These are seldom if ever reproduced in the English. Yet the tone of voice makes a deal of difference in what is said. We say, "He is a nice fellow," and the one who hears believes it. If we emphasize the verb and put a falling inflection on the adjective and say the same words, the one who hears does not believe it.

Here is a little child, just able to toddle; and we say to him, in the sweetest of tones, "You wretched little scamp, you: we will have to spank you," and the little "scamp" toddles right into our arms; but when we put on a frown and speak gruffly and say, "You sweet little darling, you; we will have to give you a stick of candy," the little darling toddles for the door as fast as he can. The tone made a deal of difference, not at all what was said. The particles in Greek measurably represent the smile or the frown, the blandness or bluster, the feature and tone; so that sometimes by their aid we almost can see the Master's face or hear the sweetness of his speech. The

English translation, the interpreter, gives only the bare, bald meaning as well as it can, without any attempt at reproducing the personality or tone.

IV. Again, the Greek emphasizes important words by their position in the sentence. The English versions emphasize nothing. The Authorized Version put into italics, not the important words, but the words which the Greek left out altogether; that is to say, the words which were of no importance in the original. Surely, it is worth while to know upon what words Jesus and Paul put their emphasis, and the Greek alone will tell that. "The Greek has very abundant resources for denoting varying shades of emphasis. One has only to examine the heroic and uncouth attempts of certain translators to represent these lights and shades by inversions and mechanical devices to see how desirable and how hopeless is the task. The sale of such books is a strong proof of the conscious need of many who cannot read the Greek and who yet understand that the knowledge of the true emphasis of the Scriptures removes difficulties, prevents false inferences, resolves many doubts, and teaches some important truths."

1. The English student of the Bible does not know how to emphasize Peter's question there

at the Last Supper: "Lord, dost thou wash my feet?" Shall we emphasize the word "my" or the word "feet"? The reader of the Greek text sees at the first glance that neither of those words is emphatic, and that the only proper reading of the sentence will put the emphasis on the word "thou."

2. How shall the English reader know how to emphasize the sentence containing the question asked by the disciples before the miracle of the multiplication of the loaves, "Whence should we have so many loaves in a desert place, as to fill so great a multitude?" We might emphasize the word "many" or the word "desert" or the word "great." Usually the English reader makes his own choice of the emphatic word in the sentence without any regard to the emphasis of the original. The Greek emphasizes the pronoun "we" in that sentence.

3. In Matt. 11. 28 the emphatic word is the personal pronoun "I": "Come unto me, all ye that labor and are heavy laden, and I will give you rest."

4. In John 8. 46 the emphasis is on the pronoun "you": "Which of you convicteth me of sin?"

5. In 1 Tim. 6. 6 the emphasis falls on the verb "is": "Godliness with contentment is

great gain." These things are apparent to the Greek student at a glance, while the reader of the English text alone has absolutely no clue to them at all.

6. It was a great help to us to know that when Jesus said, "I say unto you, that he will avenge them speedily,"[19] he put the emphasis on that closing word "speedily." The clue to many an interpretation of Scripture is to be found speedily and satisfactorily by one glance at the emphasis indicated clearly in the Greek but seldom or never translated into the English.

V. Again and again the reader of the Greek finds some flash of light on some passage with which he has been long familiar in the English, but the English of which never had suggested the new truth the original has made plain.

1. In Heb. 11. 35 we read, "Others were tortured, not accepting their deliverance," and that translation in the English leaves us absolutely in the dark as to the mode of torture endured; but when we come upon the sentence in the Greek we see not only that they were tortured but how they were tortured as well. The verb is ἐτυμπανίσθησαν, from τύμπανον, a drum or a drumstick, then, a cudgel or heavy

---
[19]Luke 18 8.

club of any kind; and it means, "They were beaten to death with bludgeons, but under that slow and terrible torture their faith never failed them. They never accepted the deliverance which was offered and was possible at any stage in that slow, brutal murder; for they were sure they would obtain a better resurrection." The real heroism of their endurance and the extraordinary triumph of their faith becomes apparent to us only in the Greek.

2. That word recalls another in our New Testament, found in "Second Peter" 3. 16. There we read, "Our beloved brother Paul . . . wrote . . . his epistles; wherein are some things hard to be understood, which the ignorant and unsteadfast wrest, as they do also the other scriptures, unto their own destruction." They wrest the scriptures. The Greek verb is στρεβλοῦσιν and it represents "an act of the greatest violence, an act of willful torturing." Its root is στρέβλη, the instrument of torture which we call the rack, upon which the criminal was stretched and by which his limbs were twisted until in his agony he was forced to say anything his tormentors may have desired him to say. We all know how worthless confessions made under such circumstances are. To escape the intolerable pain any but the most indomitable spirits will agree to

anything the Grand Inquisitors may demand. The rack twisted lies out of people as often as it twisted the truth.

That is the picture of the Greek text. These persons put the words of the Pauline Epistles and of the other scriptures upon the rack and there tortured them and twisted them until they said anything their tormentors desired them to say. The plain sense was distorted, and the sense thus extracted was crippled and unreliable. It was more often false than true. How much fuller of meaning that text becomes when we see the picture suggested by the Greek.

We might make an indefinite list of these picture words in the Greek.

3. Take that word ὑπακοή, which we translate "obedience, submission." The picture of the Greek is that of one sitting under the feet of the Master and listening eagerly and sympathetically to all he has to say. Emerson suggested a golden phrase by which it might be translated when he said, "Our one need is to obey, and by lowly listening we shall hear the right word, the word that gives us life." Lowly listening! that is the picture of the Greek, the submissive listening which leads to obedience and life, the listening of Mary at the Master's feet.

THE GREEK TESTAMENT 197

"The submission of man's nothing perfect to God's all-complete,
As by each new obeisance in spirit I climb to his feet."

The First Epistle of Peter is full of words which are condensed metaphors.

4. In the first chapter we read of things which the angels desire to "look into." Lumby says, "'Look into' is a feeble expression whereby to render παρακύψαι. In the Greek is pictorially expressed the bent body and the outstretched neck of one who is stooping and straining to gaze on some sight which calls for wonder. Now, except in the Epistle of James, where the same word is used of the earnest gaze of the believer into the perfect law of liberty, this verb is employed only here and in the two accounts of the visit of Peter and John to the sepulcher on the morning of the resurrection. Both evangelists, Luke and John, employ the same word, and its use may be due to Peter's narration, which was given to the rest of the apostles on their return.

"The word is exactly descriptive of what he had seen, as John had reached the sepulcher before him and had paused there to look in. It was the most pictorial and expressive word he could apply to the bowed head and earnest gaze of his fellow disciple as he stooped down and looked into the empty tomb. In that vacant grave John saw what angels had longed to see. Its vacancy was the seal of man's salvation, the beginning of the glories which followed the sufferings of Christ, the keynote of the gospel which proclaimed, through that resurrection, the rising again of all the dead. In thought Peter seems by this word to have gone back to that scene by the grave of the Lord, and to have before him John's eager and astonished act and gaze while he bent down that his eyes might make sure of the truth of such things as the angels desired to see."[20] The vivid verb makes the clear picture.

5. We read in our version, "For so is the will of God, that by well-doing you should put to silence the ignorance of foolish men."[21] The verb which Peter uses in the latter clause is φιμόω, which means "to muzzle." Foolish men are to have their mouths shut by the good conduct of the Christians. All who would bark at them or bite them must find themselves muzzled by their welldoing. As a muzzle renders an ill-tempered cur harmless, so their consistent behavior must render harmless the most malicious of their foes. The Greek puts a very vivid picture before us in

---
[20] Lumby, in *Expositor, First Series*, vol. iv, pp. 117–118.
[21] 1 Pet. 2. 15.

THE GREEK TESTAMENT 199

the stead of that commonplace English translation.

6. Peter says that Christ left us an "example," and the word he uses is ὑπογραμμός, a copy-head. As a fair copy is set at the head of the page and the schoolboy writes under it his awkward attempts at reproduction and he does it over and over again until his imitation begins to look something like the example set before him, so we are to see, in Christ, the perfect example for our lives and we are to endeavor to reproduce his life in our own, and however imperfect our first attempts may be we are to keep at it patiently until at last we can approximate in some measure the model he has given. That is all suggested in the one word Peter has used, and the definiteness of the picture is wholly lost in the English translation.

7. Peter writes again, "Let none of you suffer as a murderer, or a thief, or an evildoer, or as a meddler in other men's matters."[22] We know what a murderer and a thief and an evildoer are, but we are not so sure about the last criminal in this list. He is represented by a single word in the original, a word which, as far as we know, was coined by Peter himself, for it seems to be peculiar to him,

---
[22] 1 Pet. 4. 15.

ἀλλοτριοεπίσκοπος. It is a long, compound word in the Greek and it means literally, "a bishop in the things belonging to another." Our versions seem to make an anticlimax of this list of criminals, for it begins with a murderer and it ends with a meddler. Surely Peter intended to make a climax out of it.

"A bishop is one in supreme authority in his diocese. If he chooses, he can interfere at any point and at any time. To be sure, if he exercises this privilege very continuously, he is sure to become very unpopular. Does Peter mean to suggest that a Christian man must not assume that he is a supreme authority and arbiter of other men's conduct and therefore feel called upon to put in his word of advice or of protest on all occasions whether it has been asked for or not? A man who does that can make himself a first-class nuisance all the time. If he puts in most of his time in overseeing and superintending his neighbors' affairs, he probably will do more harm than good to his neighbors and he will make the Christian profession unpopular to a degree.

"Peter may have concluded in the latter part of his life that Christians ought to keep their noses out of what did not concern them and keep their eyes off those things which it might be just as well for them not to see. They need

THE GREEK TESTAMENT 201

not be kill-joys on every occasion. Their zeal must not outrun their discretion. It might be comparatively easy for them to refrain from murder and from thieving and from any other patent evil of that sort, and it might be more difficult for them to avoid all extravagances of pious profession and all inopportunities of remonstrance among their heathen neighbors; but if they achieved the last, they would help the Christian cause along more rapidly than they could in any other way.

"A too zealous Christian might overdo the thing and do much harm. A too cautious Christian might underdo the thing and miss many an opportunity for doing good. A discreet Christian would pursue the middle course and be admired of all men as a rare specimen of good sense and consecration. Peter had had many a sad experience as the result of his own impetuous interference in other men's affairs in his earlier days, and he had come to consider that prudence at this point was a supreme virtue in the Christian life. When he had intermeddled with the Master's affairs at Cæsarea Philippi he had been called a devil and the prince of devils for his pains. In these latter days he had come to believe that such interference was the superlative sin. He coins this remarkable word and puts it as the climax of his sentence, because it presented such a definite picture to his own mind, and a glance at his newly coined Greek compound is full of suggestion to us."[23]

8. A college class was reading one day in the Gospel according to Matthew and it came to the sentence, "And whosoever shall compel thee to go one mile, go with him twain."[24] When the teacher told the class that the command had a local and specific application and that "the Persian arrangements respecting post messages, instituted by Cyrus, justified the couriers, the king's officers, in making requisitions from station to station of men or cattle or carriages for the carrying on of their journey," the boys said that they never had heard of that explanation, and he was astonished; for the Greek verb bears its meaning so plainly written on its face that he who runs may read. The title of the couriers or king's officers was ἄγγαροι, and the Greek verb was ἀγγαρεύειν, to be pressed into the king's service as an ἄγγαρος; but the boys who had been students of the English Testament all their lives did not know that.

There is no need to multiply these illustrations. Every page of the Greek Testament

---
[23]Hayes, *New Testament Epistles*, pp. 173–174.
[24]Matt. 5. 41.

will furnish them. Enough has been said to make it clear that everyone who desires to have that accurate and satisfactory knowledge which alone can make him worthy of the office of an expounder of the Scripture must be able to read for himself the Word of God as first spoken and written, must reach Divine Truth for himself and not through an interpreter. There is so little exposition of the Scriptures in some pulpits to-day because the man in the pulpit knows how deficient he is in the knowledge of the original tongues of the Bible and therefore how little he is qualified to expound its truth with any authority.

It is easier to preach on current events or to make an oratorical display or to deliver a moral or philosophical or scientific lecture than it is to master the Word of God either in the English or in the original. There are learned French and German and English antagonists of the Christian who are perfectly at home in the Hebrew and the Greek and when they make their attacks and quote the original to substantiate their positions the man who knows nothing about these Bible languages can make no reply. He always must depend upon others for his answers. He can repeat only what he has heard others say. He never can be an authority. He never can speak with certainty. He always must have a feeling of inadequacy and inferiority.

First-hand knowledge of the Word will be the only knowledge which will prove always sufficient. Without it a preacher or teacher or any Christian is more or less at the mercy of every impostor who comes along. Without it a Christian student is more or less at a loss to answer the thousand and one questions which any comparison of the Authorized and the Revised Versions will suggest to the youngest or most illiterate inquirer; but with it he will have a knowledge "like him, who, at last after a long journey, sees with his own eyes and walks with his own feet the country where the Word was made flesh! A knowledge to restore to every gospel narrative new touches of reality, to every New Testament saying added fervor and freshness. A knowledge by which one may understand not only what the Lord and the apostles said, but also how they said it. A knowledge . . . divinely opportune and commanding. Verily, a knowledge worth toiling and praying for, and, finally gained, even in part, to thank God for."

This knowledge can be obtained for one hour's study a day for three years. Anybody can have it who is willing to pay the price.

1. We recall the inspiring example of Gran-

THE GREEK TESTAMENT 205

ville Sharp. Every freedman and every descendant of freedmen owes an incalculable debt to Granville Sharp. He began the movement which Clarkson and Wilberforce and Brougham afterward helped along to its triumphant issue, the abolition of slavery on British soil. In the beginning Granville Sharp stood alone. "With all the courts in the realm against him, he started out to secure a decision that no man could be a slave anywhere in the British possessions. Fighting his case up to the highest tribunal, in spite of all odds, and with no seeming advantages, he overturned all former judicial decisions, wrested from the eminent Lord Chief-Justice Mansfield an admission of previous error, and secured the promulgation of the decision he had sought—that no person could be held as a slave on the soil of Great Britain."

That was the man who was told in an argument that his ignorance of the Greek made him incompetent to discuss intelligently the doctrine of the deity of Jesus. Granville Sharp did not know whether that statement was a true one or not. The only way to find out was to study the language. So he set about the mastery of the Greek. He was not willing to be silenced in argument by an opponent's assumption of superior knowledge because of an acquaintance with an ancient tongue. He became a Greek scholar, and his work on the Greek Article which led to the more elaborate treatises of Middleton and Wordsworth is said to have marked a new epoch in New Testament exegesis.

2. John Brown of Haddington was a poor shepherd lad in the hills of Scotland. He was an orphan and had only the most meager education. By extraordinary effort he attained to some knowledge of Latin, and then he became ambitious to master the Greek. He had no instructor and he had to make his own grammar and his own lexicon, beginning by puzzling out the alphabet from the proper names in the genealogies of Jesus given in the Gospel according to Matthew and the Gospel according to Luke, which he found in a borrowed copy of the New Testament in Greek. He was anxious to have a Greek Testament of his own and he left his flocks with a friend one night and walked twenty-four miles to Saint Andrews, arriving in the morning in time for the opening of the bookshop there. In the afternoon he was back again with his sheep, studying his own Greek New Testament as he tended the flock. He was just sixteen years of age when he acquired this treasure, and he lived to be the greatest scholar in his church;

THE GREEK TESTAMENT 207

and some of his books have been published and republished for two centuries since. His Self-Interpreting Bible was reissued in America in 1919 and has had twenty-six editions in all.

3. When a boy in his teens Henry Schliemann was working from five in the morning to eleven at night in a grocery store as clerk. One day a university graduate who had become drunken and dissolute came into the store and recited about a hundred lines from Homer. "From that moment," wrote Schliemann afterward, "I never ceased to pray God that, by his grace, I might yet have the happiness of learning Greek." Where there is a will there is a way. He learned ancient and modern Greek, Dutch, English, French, Italian, Spanish, Portuguese, Swedish, Polish, Arabic, and Russian. He made those excavations at Troy and at Mycenæ which led the learned world to heap their honors upon him. He died world-famous and worth some millions of dollars. He lived in the later years of his life in Greek style in a noble palace in Athens. He named his children Andromache and Agamemnon. No other language than Greek was spoken in the household or allowed at the table, unless some guest was present whose deficiencies in Greek made some other language a courteous necessity.

4. Julia Ward Howe was seventy years old when she began the study of Greek, and in two years' time she was able to read Sophocles in the original with great enjoyment.

5. Erasmus was a poor boy at the University of Paris, working his way through school. He wrote to a friend, "I have given up my whole soul to Greek learning, and as soon as I can get any money I shall buy Greek books and then clothes." He became the great Greek scholar of the Reformation period and the acknowledged greatest authority in the field of scholarship in Europe.

6. John Knox studied Greek when he was over fifty years of age.

7. Hetty Wesley was a brilliant, fascinating girl, full of mischief but rarely gifted in intellect, and we are told that she read her Greek Testament when she was only eight years old. She must have been something like Professor James Adam, who says that when he was just a lad he was extraordinarily attracted to the Greek, "the letters looked so nice" to him, and he used to pace up and down the garden walks, devouring the Greek grammar. She delighted in it in like manner.

8. Elizabeth Barrett Browning was another rarely gifted woman and possibly the greatest of all the women poets of England. She was

THE GREEK TESTAMENT 209

addicted to the study of Greek from her earliest youth. She says, "The Greeks were my demigods, and haunted me out of Pope's Homer, until I dreamt more of Agamemnon than of Moses, my black pony. . . . The love of Pope's Homer threw me into Pope on one side and into Greek on the other, and into Latin as a help to Greek. . . . I had fits of Pope and Byron and Coleridge, and read Greek as hard under the trees as some of your Oxonians under the Bodleian; gathered visions from Plato and the dramatists, and ate and drank Greek and made my head ache with it." That was her preparation for her life work.

9. She married Robert Browning, the greatest poet of his age and another devoted student of the Greek masters. On his study table lay a little Greek Bible, on the last leaf of which he had written, "My wife's book and mine." It was one of his greatest treasures, the book from which his wife and he always had read the Scriptures.

10. We are told that John Stuart Blackie never spent a day without reading, translating, and pondering a passage from the Greek Testament, and he wore out many copies of the book.

11. The greatest evangelical preacher of the

last century in England was Charles Haddon Spurgeon. He felt it incumbent upon him in preparation for efficient ministry to make himself familiar with Hebrew and Greek. He was not content until he knew them.

12. The greatest expository preacher of the last century in England was Alexander Maclaren. He attributed his success in the exposition of the Scriptures to his hard work at the Hebrew Bible and the Greek Testament. He began it in school but he continued it through the after years of his ministry. He never let a day pass without reading at least one chapter in both the Hebrew and the Greek. At one time he said: "A minute study of the mere words of Scripture, though it may seem like grammatical trifling and pedantry, yields large results. Men do sometimes gather grapes of thorns; and the hard, dry work of trying to get at the precise shade of meaning in Scripture words always repays with large lessons and impulses."

In any one of his books we can find illustrations of this truth. We pick up the volume entitled *After the Resurrection,* and open it at random near the middle of the book. He is discussing the phrase, "Kept by the power of God," and he says, "If we render quite literally, we shall say, 'Kept in the power of God.'

Though the 'by' is a perfectly legitimate explanation of the apostle's meaning, do you not see how much more beauty and picturesque force is given, if we say 'kept or guarded in the power of God,' as if it were round about us, and we were there in the midst? 'The name of the Lord is a strong tower, the righteous runneth into it and is safe.' 'He that dwelleth in the secret place of the Most High' and that does not mean the secret place that belongs to the Most High, but the secret place that the Most High constitutes—'He that dwelleth in the secret place of the Most High shall abide under the shadow'—yes, of course he will; if he is close in, he is sure to be below the shadow—'of the Almighty.'

"Similarly, taking the same metaphor as is in my text, 'The angel of the Lord' (not the angels), 'the angel of the Lord encampeth round about them that fear him, and they are kept in the power.' When an army is marching through an enemy's country, they put the women and children and invalids in the center, and then they are safe; and that is where you and I will be safe—inserted into God, if I may venture upon such a phrase. It is not too strong a phrase; it is not half so strong as the Master's 'Abide in me and I in you, for apart from me ye'—not merely 'can do,' but ye—'are nothing.' "[25] These are the comments of one who has lingered lovingly upon the words of the original and has found in them many a truth not suggested by any translation.

We turn over a few pages in this volume and we find the author saying, "The word rendered 'patience' does not mean merely the passive virtue of endurance, but involves likewise the notion of active persistence and perseverance in a given course, irrespective of the obstacles, the sorrows and difficulties, which may threaten to hinder our advance. Brave perseverance, much rather than quiet endurance, is the meaning of the word."[26]

Just a few pages farther on we read again: "Do not forget either that when we say 'good works,' we only partially represent the depth of the apostle's meaning here, for he employs, as many of you know, that profound and lovely Greek phraseology by which, instead of describing the acts as 'good'—an adjective which only defines their moral quality—he qualifies them as 'beautiful,' an adjective which implies the appeal which they make to every man's sense of harmony, of loveliness, of symmetry, of proportionateness. All 'good' works are

---

[25] Maclaren, *After the Resurrection*, pp. 176–177. George H. Doran Company. Used by permission.

[26] Maclaren, *op. cit.*, p. 235.

beautiful. Alas! that the earthliness and sensuality of men have degraded and besmirched art so that we cannot say all beautiful work is good. Let us take this lesson: that nothing comes up to the Christian standard, however conformed it may be morally to the great law of rectitude, unless it is conformed also to the no less imperative law of beauty; and that we are just as much bound to seek to make our lives fair, as we are bound to make them pure."[27]

We turn a few more pages and we find him talking about the Master's graciousness to the woman who was a sinner and who had anointed his feet at Simon's feast, and he says that Jesus did not say to her, "'Go in peace,' as our Versions have it, but 'Go into peace,' and that is a great deal more than the other. 'Go in peace' refers to the momentary emotion; 'Go into peace' seems, as it were, to open the door of a great palace, to let down the barrier on the borders of a land, and to send the person away upon a journey through all the extent of that blessed country. . . . Remember that this commandment, which is likewise a promise and a bestowal, bids us progress in the peace into which Christ admits us. We should be growingly unperturbed and calm,

---
[27]Maclaren, *op. cit.*, p. 243.

and 'there is no joy but calm,' when all is said and done. We should be more and more tranquil and at rest; and every day there should come as it were a deeper and more substantial layer of tranquillity enveloping our hearts, a thicker armor against perturbation and calamity and tumult."[28]

These pages could be paralleled in any of the many volumes of sermons and expositions published by Alexander Maclaren, and we quote them not as unusual specimens of exegesis but as samples of his ordinary and habitual practice in sermonizing. He went to the original text to get the meaning of the writers at first hand, and this was one element of his freshness and fertility through the decades of his ministry. Joseph Parker said of him, "There is no greater preacher than Alexander Maclaren in the English-speaking pulpit," and Hugh Price Hughes declared, "He is the highest modern exponent from the pulpit of the spoken Word."

13. There are many people who think that Phillips Brooks was the greatest preacher of America in his generation. When he was in the theological school at Alexandria, Virginia, he did not much enjoy the Hebrew. He wrote concerning it, "Hebrew is a tough old tongue,

---
[28]Maclaren, *op. cit.*, pp. 253-254, 255-256.

THE GREEK TESTAMENT 215

as independent as these thirteen United States, so that no little previous knowledge of any other language helps one out at all in his dealings with it." However, one of his friends said of him: "Though he never took very kindly to Hebrew, as a classical scholar none matched him. . . . The Greek of the New Testament Epistles as he dealt with it 'rejoiced like Enoch in being translated.'"

14. J. H. Jowett and G. Campbell Morgan have continued this tradition of scholarly exegesis based upon the original text in the English and American pulpit of to-day. Through the ages the great preachers have had the power of fluent translation and ready comprehension of the original text. All the great onward movements in church history have been due to students of the Greek.

15. In the beginning, when the infant church was content to stay in Jerusalem and Palestine, and to preach only to Jews, the Jewish prejudices and antipathies fostered for ages being dominant still, in that crisis a young man born in Tarsus, at that time one of the three world centers of Greek learning and culture, educated in the schools of Tarsus, superior in this period, as Strabo declares, to the schools of either Athens or Alexandria, a young man of Jewish race and Greek educa-

tion was let loose upon the nations and preached to the Greeks in Ephesus and Thessalonica and Corinth and Athens the gospel of world-wide import, and founded among them some of the strongest of his churches. Christianity captured Greece and allied itself with Greek culture, and in the end that fact gave it the victory over Mithraism, its only serious rival in the ancient world.

16. Centuries later, when the darkness of the Middle Ages had settled over all Europe, the darkness of dense ignorance upon the mass of the population, the darkness of religious despotism and dogmatism through all the Roman Catholic Church, Constantinople fell, its Greek scholars and their Greek manuscripts with them were scattered through all the farther West, and when with Greek culture there came the Revival of Learning, the first result was Luther's and Tyndale's and Calvin's revival of religion as well in the Great Reformation. All these leaders knew Greek and based their exposition and preaching upon the truth of the original text. "Greece rose from the dead with the New Testament in her hands," and behold, all things became new in its power.

17. Again, when formalism had taken the place of faith in England and the Continent and the illuminating and purifying fires of

THE GREEK TESTAMENT 217

Methodism were set aglow in all the lands, the leader in this last great onward movement of religious life and church activity was a Fellow of Oxford University and a lecturer on Greek, the author of a translation of the Greek New Testament which antedates nearly all the excellences of the Revised Versions by more than a century and a quarter. John Wesley was a never-tiring student of the Greek original of the gospel which he preached, like Paul, to his parish, the world. Methodism was born in a university, and in the beginning all the Methodists read Greek. Bishop Simpson once said, "A half dozen students and tutors in the university, studying the word of God critically, believing it implicitly, and obeying it practically in every possible form of doing good—this was old-fashioned Methodism."

The primitive Methodists pored over the pages of the Greek New Testament. The founder of that church was proud to call himself *homo unius libri,* a man of one book; and the book which he cherished above all others and with which he was most familiar was the Greek New Testament. Bishop Hendrix says, "His Greek Testament was his constant companion on land and water, and all his life he was able to quote from the original any text of Scripture whose English rendering in the King James Version he had for the moment forgotten." We read that upon the naming of any word in the Greek Testament he would immediately tell every passage in which the word occurred, with all its uses, and in all its various connections. That sounds apocryphal, but it doubtless was true of many words in the New Testament, if not of all.

This is the man who wrote that "Address to the Clergy," in which he insisted upon a knowledge on their part of both Hebrew and Greek. "A guide to souls ought to know the literal meaning of every word, verse, and chapter in Scripture; without which there can be no firm foundation on which the spiritual meaning can be built. . . . Can he do this, in the most effectual manner, without a knowledge of the original tongues? Without this will he not frequently be at a stand, even as to texts which regard practice only? But he will be under still greater difficulties, with respect to controverted scriptures. He will be ill able to rescue these out of the hands of any man of learning that would pervert them: for whenever an appeal is made to the original, his mouth is stopped at once."[29]

Later in that Address he comes to close

---
[29] Wesley, *Works*, vol. vi, p. 218.

THE GREEK TESTAMENT 219

quarters in a series of interrogations. "Do I understand Greek and Hebrew? Otherwise, how can I undertake (as every minister does), not only to explain books which are written therein but to defend them against all opponents? Am I not at the mercy of everyone who does understand, or even pretends to understand the original? For which way can I confute his pretense? Do I understand the language of the Old Testament? critically? at all? Can I read into English one of David's psalms; or even the first chapter of Genesis? Do I understand the language of the New Testament? Am I a critical master of it? Have I enough of it even to read into English the first chapter of Saint Luke? If not, how many years did I spend at school? How many at the university? And what was I doing all those years? Ought not shame to cover my face?"[30]

Mr. Herrick says: "John Wesley was the peer in his literary attainments of any literary character of that most literary period. No gownsman of the university, no lawned and mitered prelate was, intellectually, the superior of this itinerating Methodist." His best scholarship was in Greek, and it is a marvel how he succeeded in making many of his help-

[30] Wesley, op. cit., p. 224.

ers equally enthusiastic and earnest in their study of that tongue.

18. Adam Clarke was worthy to stand by Wesley's side as a Greek scholar and exegete. We are told that he had every kind of diploma which represented the learning and the scholarship of his day. If he had so chosen he had the right to add twenty-two letters after his name to represent his unsought but well-merited titles. He had what he called his portable library which he carried with him on his journeys. There were seven books in that library, which he thus kept always with him. Those seven books were the Hebrew Bible, the Septuagint, the Greek Testament, the English Bible, the Common Prayer Book, Virgil, and Horace. He carried the authoritative texts with him wherever he went.

19. Bishop Coke tells us in his *Journal* that when he was crossing the ocean to organize the Methodist Church in America the Greek Testament was his constant and cherished companion.

20. "The well-worn Greek Testament of Captain Webb is still preserved as a precious and suggestive relic.

21. "Even Asbury, the apostolic pioneer bishop of American Methodism, the very embodiment of tireless energy in evangelistic

THE GREEK TESTAMENT 221

work, forged by himself those keys of sacred learning which would unlock for him the treasures of the Scriptures in Hebrew and Greek." John Wesley and his fellow laborers had great grace; but they had Greek as well as grace and God's more abundant blessing was upon them.

The proved existence of a more blessed state of experience and the proved possibility of attainment thereto lays the striving therefor as an imperative duty upon every believing soul. Acquaintance with the Greek Testament is a more blessed state of experience than dense ignorance respecting it. Any Christian can give one hour a day for three years to his Greek Testament, if he really cares to do so. It is an imperative duty then to do it. After all, our Christian religion draws its inspiration from sources which are accessible only in Greek, and the study of Greek is essential to any first-hand access to these sources. That fact alone would make it desirable for every Christian minister and layman to study Greek.

Add to that fact the probability that his experience would be like that of President James, of the University of Illinois, who said, "Aside from English, I have always thought that I got more power of drawing fine distinctions, of seeing things clearly, of expressing myself so that other people could understand me, of insight into certain phases of human life and human history, and of inspiration for everything that was worth while being inspired for, out of my Greek study than out of any other single study extending over a similar length of time and taking a similar amount of energy."[31] If the study itself should prove to be thus pleasurable and profitable and inspiring for everything which was worth being inspired for, the process as well as the result would be well worth the effort required.

We have read of one who had lost his interest in the New Testament because of his very familiarity with the English version of it. He said that endless repetition had spoiled the freshness and charm of the book for him. He was a good Greek student, and one day he took up the Greek Testament and he found it a new and delightful book in the original. He said it was like going into a garden of lilies out of some dark and narrow house.

Postscript Number 1

If anyone should think of studying the Greek language, the following suggestions may be helpful:

---

[31]West, *op. cit.*, pp 187–188.

THE GREEK TESTAMENT 223

1. It is desirable to have a teacher in the beginning, if possible.

2. If neither class instruction nor a private tutor is available, a correspondence course can be taken with the University of Chicago or Columbia University, or any other institution providing such work.

3. There are excellent manuals for beginners in New Testament Greek, such as Harper and Weidner's *Introductory New Testament Greek Method,* Davis' *Beginner's Grammar of the Greek New Testament,* or Huddilston's *Essentials of New Testament Greek.*

4. Any good grammar of classical Greek will serve all needs.

5. The best grammars of New Testament Greek are Winer–Moulton, J. H. Moulton, Blass, and A. T. Robertson.

6. For New Testament Lexicons, either Thayer or Abbott–Smith will be sufficient.

7. Liddell and Scott or any good lexicon of classical Greek will serve for all Greek literature.

POSTSCRIPT NUMBER 2

The author desires to express his appreciation of the courtesy extended him by the following publishers and individuals in granting permission to quote from books copyrighted by them:

D. Appleton & Company. Darwin, *Descent of Man.* Gulick, *Life of the Ancient Greeks.* Huxley, *Science and Culture.* Lecky, *History of European Morals.*

The Century Co. Butler, *The Story of Athens.*

Clarendon Press, Oxford. Hatch, *Essays in Biblical Greek*. Livingstone, *Pageant of Greece*.

Congregational Publishing Society. Burton, *In Pulpit and Parish*.

George H. Doran Company. Alexander, *The Epistles of John*. Maclaren, *Exposition of the Holy Scripture*. Robertson, *The Minister and the New Testament*.

E. P. Dutton & Company. Mill, *Dissertations*.

Harvard University Press. Greene, *Achievement of Greece*.

Henry Holt and Company. Gildersleeve, *Hellas and Hesperia*.

Houghton Mifflin Company. Ballentine, *Riverside New Testament*. Shairp, *Culture and Religion*.

Longmans, Green & Co. Farrar, *Greek Syntax*. Mill, *Representative Government*.

P. M. Martin. *Is Mankind Advancing?*

Princeton University Press. West, *Value of the Classics*.

Charles Scribner's Sons. *Makers of Hellas*. Briggs, *The Study of Holy Scripture*. Hastings' *Bible Dictionary*. Jowett, *Dialogues of Plato*. Schaff, *History of the Apostolic Church*.

Yale University Press. Cooper, *The Greek Genius and Its Influence*.

www.ingramcontent.com/pod-product-compliance
Lightning Source LLC
Chambersburg PA
CBHW062026220426
43662CB00010B/1486